LawExpress
ENGLISH LEGAL SYSTEM

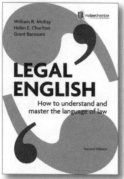

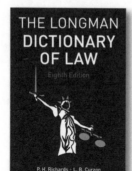
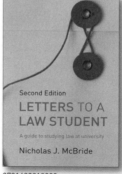

Law Express

ENGLISH LEGAL SYSTEM

4th edition

Emily Finch
Senior Lecturer in Law, University of Surrey

Stefan Fafinski
Research Associate of Oxford Internet Institute

PEARSON

Harlow • England • London • New York • Boston • San Francisco • Toronto • Sydney • Auckland • Singapore • Hong Kong
Tokyo • Seoul • Taipei • New Delhi • Cape Town • São Paulo • Mexico City • Madrid • Amsterdam • Munich • Paris • Milan

Pearson Education Limited
Edinburgh Gate
Harlow
Essex CM20 2JE
England

and Associated Companies throughout the world

Visit us on the World Wide Web at:
www.pearson.com/uk

First published 2007
Second edition published 2009
Third edition published 2010
Fourth edition published 2013

ISBN: 978-1-4082-9537-3

British Library Cataloguing-in-Publication Data
A catalogue record for this book is available from the British Library

Library of Congress Cataloging-in-Publication Data
Finch, Emily.
  English legal system / Emily Finch, Stefan Fafinski. — 4th ed.
    p. cm.
  Includes index.
  ISBN 978-1-4082-9537-3 (pbk.)
  1. Law—England. I. Fafinski, Stefan. II. Title.
  KD661.F565 2012
  349.42—dc23

                          2012015645

10 9 8 7 6 5 4 3 2
15 14 13

Typeset in *Helvetica Neue LT Pro 10/12 pt*
Printed and bound by *Ashford Colour Press Ltd., Gosport*

WESTON
COLLEGE
LIBRARY

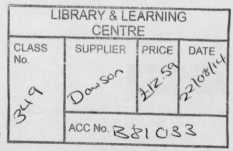

Contents

Supporting resources

Visit the Law Express series companion website at **www.pearsoned.co.uk/ lawexpress** to find valuable student learning material including:

- A study plan test to assess how well you know the subject before you begin your revision, now broken down into targeted study units
- Interactive quizzes with a variety of question types to test your knowledge of the main points from each chapter of the book
- Further examination questions and guidelines for answering them
- Interactive flashcards to help you revise the main terms and cases
- Printable versions of the topic maps and checklists
- 'You be the marker' allows you to see exam questions and answers from the perspective of the examiner and includes notes on how an answer might be marked
- Podcasts provide point-by-point instruction on how to answer a common exam question

Also: The companion website provides the following features:

- Search tool to help locate specific items of content
- E-mail results and profile tools to send results of quizzes to instructors
- Online help and support to assist with website usage and troubleshooting

For more information please contact your local Pearson Education sales represent- ative or visit **www.pearsoned.co.uk/lawexpress**

Acknowledgements

This book is dedicated to STG.

We are, as ever, grateful to all who have offered feedback on the last edition of *Law Express: English Legal System*, particularly the anonymous academic reviewers who provided some suggestions for improvement. We have been pleased to incorporate these as best we could.

Emily Finch and Stefan Fafinski
Wokingham

Publisher's acknowledgements

Our thanks go to all reviewers who contributed to the development of this text, including students who participated in research and focus groups which helped to shape the series format.

Introduction

A thorough understanding of the English legal system is vital for law students. It sets the foundations upon which all other legal study is based. It also introduces students to the 'tools of the trade' – specifically, how to read, understand and apply case law and statute law; how the court system works and who fulfils the various roles associated with the administration of justice. Equipped with this knowledge, students will be well placed to cover all other areas of the law.

Since study of the English legal system underpins other legal study, it is usually taught at the start of the overall course. This presents some unique problems – the subject is typically encountered by students experiencing their first taste of undergraduate level law, who are only just beginning to learn how to think, write and analyse like lawyers. Therefore, you will need greater help in beginning to formulate your essay-writing and problem-solving technique. This book will aim to give you some guidance in those areas in specific relation to the English legal system. If you have already studied law at A-level, don't fall into the trap that so many students do of assuming that you've 'done all this before' and neglecting your studies on English legal systems in favour of some newer or seemingly more exciting topics: the level required of an undergraduate is higher and you will be expected to go into greater depth than in previous study.

This revision guide is just what it says – a guide to *revision*. It is not a substitute for attendance at lectures and seminars; it does not provide an excuse not to read and follow your own course materials and textbooks; it should not cut down on the amount of reading and thinking that you have to do. The English legal system is a vast and complex subject – you should be able to realise that from looking at the size of your recommended textbook. It follows that a revision guide such as this could never be expected to cover the subject in the depth required to succeed in exams, and it does not set out to do so. Instead, it aims to provide a concise overview of the key areas for revision – reminding you of the headline points to enable you to focus your revision and identify the key points you need to know.

While there are outline answers to the questions within the book and on the website, we have purposely avoided providing 'model' answers. It is important that you develop your own approach to answering questions based on knowledge and understanding rather than on memory. Also, it is very unlikely that you will be asked *exactly* the same question in an exam; you must always try to answer the precise question set, not something closely related but different in focus.

A further word of warning – the English legal system is a very broad topic. Unlike some other areas of the law, the material covered from institution to institution can vary greatly. This book attempts to cover the most common areas. However, you may find that there are topics in this book that are not covered on your particular course; that there are topics on your course that are not covered in this book; or that there are topics in this book that are covered in much greater depth on your course. Therefore, you *must* make sure that you are fully aware of the content of your own course before beginning to revise, and to use this book with care for what it is – a signpost to the major areas you will need to revise in order to do well.

Finally, note that the 'English legal system' is a convenient label – remember that it currently extends to both England *and Wales.* Scotland, the Isle of Man and the Channel Islands have separate systems.

📖 **REVISION NOTE**

Things to bear in mind when revising the English legal system:

- If you have encountered the subject before, don't assume you know it all.
- Do rely on this book to help guide your revision.
- Don't simply rely on this book to tell you everything you need to know.
- Make sure you have your syllabus to hand.
- Make use of your lecture notes, textbooks and other materials as you revise – this will ensure you understand the subject in depth – which is the only way to do well.
- Take every opportunity to practise your essay-writing and problem-solving technique: get as much feedback as you can.
- Many topics in this book are linked – the English legal system as a subject provides almost unlimited scope for cunning examiners to cover more than one topic in a single question – if you choose to revise selectively, you could easily find yourself caught out.

Before you begin, you can use the study plan available on the companion website to assess how well you know the material in this book and identify the areas where you may want to focus your revision.

Guided tour

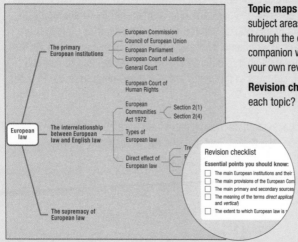

Topic maps – Visual guides highlight key subject areas and facilitate easy navigation through the chapter. Download them from the companion website to pin on your wall or add to your own revision notes.

Revision checklists – How well do you know each topic? Use these to identify essential points you should know for your exams. But don't panic if you don't know them all - the chapters will help you revise each point to ensure you are fully prepared. Print the checklists off the companion website and track your revision progress!

Sample questions with answer guidelines – Practice makes perfect! Read the question at the start of each chapter and consider how you would answer it. Guidance on structuring strong answers is provided at the end of the chapter. Try out additional sample questions online.

Assessment advice – Not sure how best to tackle a problem or essay question? Wondering what you may be asked? Use the assessment advice to identify the ways in which a subject may be examined and how to apply your knowledge effectively.

Key definitions – Make sure you understand essential legal terms. Use the flashcards online to test your recall!

■ Sample question

Could you answer this question? Below is a typical problem question that could arise on this topic. Guidelines on answering the question are included at the end of the chapter, whilst a sample essay question and guidance on tackling it can be found on the companion website.

ASSESSMENT ADVICE

Within the context of an English Legal system course, it is still possible to encounter both essay and problem questions which concern the operation or impact of European law.

Essay questions

Typically take one of two approaches, either requiring a discussion of the impact that European law has had on the English legal system, or as part of a more general question on sources of law, of which European law forms one part (along with domestic legislation and law made through judicial interpretation or the operation of the doctrine of precedent).

Problem questions

Typically take the form of a series of pieces of (often fictitious) European legislation which are potentially relevant to a problem scenario. You are then asked to analyse whether or not they apply, and if so, why and with what effect. This may be combined with other matters of statutory interpretation or precedent. In a question like this, a detailed understanding of horizontal and vertical direct effect is essential.

KEY DEFINITIONS: Vertical and horizontal direct effect

A provision of European law has *vertical* direct effect if it is enforceable against a member state in its own courts. In the United Kingdom this means that vertically directly effective provisions can be enforced against the United Kingdom itself, as well as against local authorities, health authorities (*Marshall* v. *Southampton and South West Hampshire Area Health Authority (No. 2)* [1994] QB 126, CJEC) and nationalised industries (*Foster* v. *British Gas plc* [1991] 1 QB 405, CJEC).

A provision of European law has *horizontal* direct effect if it can be enforced against another individual.

Key cases and key statutes – Identify and review the important elements of the essential cases and statutes you will need to know for your exams.

> **KEY CASE**
>
> *Van Gend en Loos v. Nederlandse Administratie der Belastingen* [1963] ECR 1, CJEC
>
> *Concerning: vertical direct effect of Treaty Articles*
>
> **KEY STATUTE**
>
> **Section 2(1) of the European C...**
>
> All such rights, powers, liabilities, or arising by or under the Treaties to time provided for by or under th without further enactment to be be recognised and available in
>
> ...ch company wanted to enforce Article 12 EEC against the Dutch customs authorities ...ad increased the duty on imports. The matter was referred to the European Court ...e.
>
> ...nciple
>
> ...y Article created individual enforceable rights against the state (i.e. it had ...direct effect) because its terms were ' clear, precise and unconditional ' and ...as no room for discretion in implementation. Its implementation required no ...r legislation in member states (i.e. it was *directly applicable*). Therefore, member ...es had no discretion in the means of its implementation. These criteria are often ...eferred to simply as the *Van Gend* criteria.

Make your answer stand out – This feature illustrates sources of further thinking and debate where you can maximise your marks. Use them to really impress your examiners!

> ✓ Make your answer stand out
>
> ■ Make sure you state the *Van Gend* criteria accurately.
> ■ Be clear why it is important for the date for implementation of the Directive to have passed.
> ■ Use the terms *vertical* and *horizontal* direct effect accurately – it is important to be precise to distinguish your answer from that of a student with a more superficial knowledge of the subject area.
> ■ Comment on the possibility of *Francovich* damages; this is often overlooked in questions involving reliance on Directives.

Exam tips – Feeling the pressure? These boxes indicate how you can improve your exam performance when it really counts.

> **EXAM TIP**
>
> It is important to remember the *Van Gend* criteria when talking about Regulations and Directives as well as Treaty Articles.

Revision notes – Get guidance for effective revision. These boxes highlight related points and areas of overlap in the subject, or areas where your course might adopt a particular approach that you should check with your course tutor.

> **REVISION NOTE**
>
> When considering the jurisdiction of the European Court of Justice and General Court, you may wish to skip forward to Chapter 3 and revisit the domestic institutions of the court system.

Don't be tempted to . . . – This feature underlines areas where students most often trip up in exams. Use them to spot common pitfalls and avoid losing marks.

> ! Don't be tempted to . . .
>
> It is vitally important not to confuse the European Court of Justice (which sits in Luxembourg) with the European Court of Human Rights (which sits in Strasbourg).
>
> It is also important not to confuse the Council of the European Union with the Council of Europe. The Council of Europe is a separate body and has responsibility for the European Court of Human Rights.

Read to impress – Focus on these carefully selected sources to extend your knowledge, deepen your understanding, and earn better marks in coursework as well as in exams.

> **READ TO IMPRESS**
>
> Craig, P. and G. de Burca (2011) *EU Law: Text, Cases and Materials*, 5th edn, Oxford: OUP.
> Fairhurst, J. (2010) *Law of the European Union*, 8th edn, Harlow: Longman.
> Weatherill, S. (2010) *Cases and Materials on EU Law*, 9th edn, Oxford: OUP.

Glossary – Forgotten the meaning of a word? This quick reference covers key definitions and other useful terms.

Glossary of terms

Guided tour of the companion website

 Book resources are available to download. Print your own **topic maps** and **revision checklists**!

 Use the **study plan** prior to your revision to help you assess how well you know the subject and determine which areas need most attention. Choose to take the full assessment or focus on targeted study units.

 'Test your knowledge' of individual areas with quizzes tailored specifically to each chapter. **Sample problem and essay questions** are also available with guidance on crafting a good answer.

 Flashcards help improve recall of important legal terms and key cases and statutes. Available in both electronic and printable formats.

'You be the marker' gives you the chance to evaluate sample exam answers for different question types and understand how and why an examiner awards marks.

Download the **podcast** and listen as your own personal Law Express tutor guides you through a 10–15 minute audio session. You will be presented with a typical but challenging question and provided with a step-by-step explanation on how to approach the question, what essential elements your answer will need for a pass, how to structure a good response, and what to do to make your answer stand out so that you can earn extra marks.

All of this and more can be found when you visit **www.pearsoned.co.uk/lawexpress**

Table of cases

Table of legislation

▮Statutes

Statutory instruments

Procedural rules

European legislation

Founding treaties

Legislation and its interpretation

1

Revision checklist

Essential points you should know:

- [ ] The process by which legislation comes into being
- [ ] The distinction between statutes and delegated legislation
- [ ] Why interpretation of legislation is necessary
- [ ] Each of the 'rules' of statutory interpretation

■ Topic map

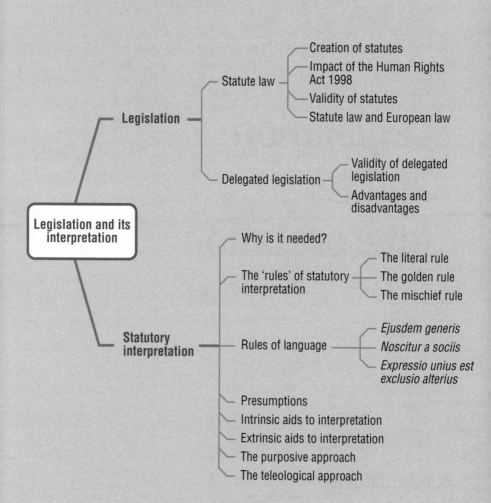

■ Introduction

Legislation is the primary source of English law, but can be open to interpretation

This chapter deals with legislation and its interpretation. An understanding of how legislation is made and how it is interpreted by the courts is an essential legal skill. Remember that virtually every legal topic will be governed in part by legislation, so the ability to analyse legislation critically will be relevant to every legal topic you study and revise, not just in isolation as a topic in the study of the English legal system. Statutory interpretation is also a popular topic for examiners as, unlike some other topics, it lends itself equally well to both problem and essay-type questions. Therefore, as you work through this chapter, think how you might use the material in both an essay and a problem situation.

ASSESSMENT ADVICE

Legislation and its interpretation is a topic that lends itself to both essay and problem questions.

Essay questions in this area will tend to require a good level of description of either the legislative process or the rules of interpretation. Remember, where you can, to illustrate your description with appropriate examples from case law. As with all essay questions, your answer will stand out if you can use the description to support an in-depth analysis of the question; a merely descriptive answer (however thorough) is unlikely to achieve high marks.

Problem questions on statutory interpretation will usually involve analysis of one or more provisions of a piece of legislation. This could be a real statute, or a piece of fictitious legislation made up to fit the particular points that the examiner is trying to bring out. It is important to be methodical and meticulous; remember to consider each of the rules, approaches and aids to interpretation in turn, even if their use seems inappropriate. Remember that the marker can only evaluate what you write down. Therefore, if you think that, for example, the literal rule would not help since it would produce a stupid outcome then say so, rather than just discounting it in your mind and moving on.

Sample question

Could you answer this question? Below is a typical essay question that could arise on this topic. Guidelines on answering the question are included at the end of the chapter, whilst a sample problem question and guidance on tackling it can be found on the companion website.

ESSAY QUESTION

'Three so-called rules of statutory interpretation have been identified . . . each originating at different stages of legal history. To call them "rules" is misleading: it is better to think of them as general approaches' (Smith, Bailey and Gunn (2002) *The Modern English Legal System*, 4th edn, London: Sweet & Maxwell, p. 409).

Discuss the above quotation in relation to the role of the judiciary.

Legislation

KEY DEFINITION: Legislation

Legislation is a broad term which covers not only *statutes* (i.e. Acts of Parliament) but other types of legislation such as *delegated* legislation, covered later in this chapter (and sometimes called **subordinate legislation**) and European legislation (see Chapter 2).

□ REVISION NOTE

When revising legislation, it may be useful (if you have covered constitutional law in another course) to refresh your memory regarding the concept of Parliamentary sovereignty. This is covered very briefly in this chapter when looking at the validity of statutes, but a more in-depth reminder now might enhance your understanding of the legislative process.

Statute law

Parliament passes **legislation** in the form of statutes, or Acts of Parliament. Such Acts will often begin as either a Public Bill, a Private Bill, or a Private Member's Bill. Bills can be introduced in the House of Commons or, less frequently, in the House of Lords.

Public Bills	Private Bills	Private Member's Bills
Introduced by the government as part of its programme of legislation	Introduced for the benefit of particular individuals, groups of people, institutions or a particular locality	Non-government Bills introduced by MPs of either House
Affect the public as a whole	Often fail to become law because of insufficient time in a particular Parliamentary session	Often deal with relatively narrow issues
	Very rare nowadays	

Statute law may also be passed to *consolidate* or *codify* the law. In addition, hybrid bills contain both public and private elements and money bills are purely financial.

KEY DEFINITION: Consolidating statute

Consolidation does *not* change the law. A consolidating statute is one in which a legal topic, previously contained in several different statutes, is re-enacted (for example, the Limitation Act 1980 and the Insolvency Act 1986).

'All consolidation Acts are designed to bring together in a more convenient, lucid and economical form a number of enactments related in subject-matter [which were] previously scattered over the statute book' – Lord Simon in *Farrell* v. *Alexander* [1977] AC 59, HL.

Codification may change the law. A **codifying statute** is one in which a legal topic, previously contained in the common law, custom and previous statute, is restated (for example, the Theft Act 1968).

Creation of statutes

Government proposals on topics of current concern are set out in *White Papers*. These signify the government's intention to enact new legislation, and may involve setting up a consultation process to consider the finer details. *Green Papers* are issued less frequently – they are introductory higher-level government reports on a particular area without any guarantee of legislative action or consideration of the legislative detail.

Stage	Comment
Commons: First reading	No resolution required. Title of Bill is read. Bill is printed and published. Minister must also state whether the Bill is compatible with Convention rights or, if not, that nevertheless the Government wishes to proceed.
Commons: Second reading	Main debate
Commons: Committee stage	Provisions examined in detail and amendments proposed
Commons: Report stage	Further debate; House votes on amendments
Commons: Third reading	Final debate and vote on Bill as amended
Proceedings in the House of Lords	Stages are as for proceedings in the House of Commons
Amendments by the House of Lords	If any amendments have been made in the House of Lords, Bill is passed back to the House of Commons after its third reading for further debate. Therefore, a Bill can go back and forth between the chambers until proceedings are terminated or the parliamentary session runs out of time. However, in practice, the Lords often accept the second offering from the House of Commons.
The Parliament Acts 1911 and 1949	These Acts provide a means by which the House of Commons can bypass the House of Lords to present a Bill for Royal Assent without it having been passed by the House of Lords (provided that the House of Lords has rejected the Bill twice). It is used infrequently (however, the Hunting Act 2004 provides a recent example of its use). See also *R (on the application of Jackson)* v. *Attorney-General* [2005] EWCA Civ 126.

Stage	Comment
Royal Assent	The Royal Assent is required before any Bill can become law. The monarch is not required by the constitution to assent to any Act passed by Parliament. However, it is conventionally given (it has not been refused since Queen Anne refused to assent to the Scottish Militia Bill of 1707). Indeed, the Royal Assent Act 1967 has marginalised the personal involvement of the monarch to the extent that all that is now required for Royal Assent is a formal reading of the short title of the Act in both Houses of Parliament.

The proposed legislation is passed to the Parliamentary draftsman (officially the 'Parliamentary Counsel to the Treasury') who drafts the Bill. The process thereafter can be depicted as shown in Figure 1.1.

Without express provision to the contrary, an Act of Parliament is deemed to come into force on the day (and for the whole of the day – *Tomlinson* v. *Bullock* (1879) 4 QBD 230, DC) that it receives Royal Assent. Otherwise, it will come into force on a date specified within the Act itself, or an 'appointed day' provision which allows the Act to be brought into force via a statutory instrument (see below). Parts of the Act may be brought into force on different dates (e.g. the provisions of the Anti-Social Behaviour Act 2003 relating to high hedges did not come into force until June 2005).

Impact of the Human Rights Act 1998

Section 19 of the Human Rights Act 1998 provides that the Minister in charge of each new Bill in either House of Parliament must, before the second reading of the Bill, either:

- make a statement of compatibility – that is, state that the provisions of the Bill are compatible with the European Convention on Human Rights; or

- make a statement acknowledging that it is not possible to make a statement of compatibility, but, despite this, the Government still wishes the House to proceed with the Bill. This is typically done on the first reading.

Moreover, the courts have *no* power to set aside any Act of Parliament that is incompatible with Convention rights; this is the prerogative of Parliament (which has a fast-track procedure which it may use in such cases if it wishes to do so).

Figure 1.1

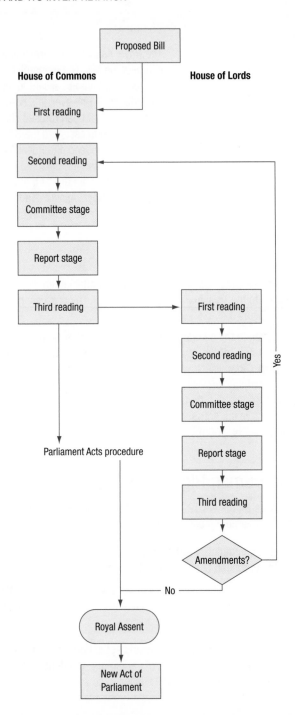

Validity of statutes

The doctrine of Parliamentary sovereignty means that the validity of any statute passed by Parliament cannot be challenged. It is most commonly associated with Dicey (1982), who defines sovereignty as consisting of:

- the right to make any law whatsoever (unlimited legislative competence), and
- the principle that there is no competing legislative body to Parliament.

In *British Railways Board* v. *Pickin* [1974] AC 765, HL, Lord Morris confirmed that the courts could not argue whether a statute 'should be on the statute book at all'. However, T.R.S. Allan (1985) has proposed that the courts should be able to challenge Acts of Parliament in exceptional circumstances (for instance, if the Act challenged the basis of democracy or was made by an unrepresentative Parliament).

 Make your answer stand out

Although Parliamentary sovereignty is a matter of constitutional law, and therefore outside the scope of most English Legal Systems courses, it is always useful to consider how it relates to the role of the courts in interpreting legislation. If Parliament is supreme, then to what extent should the courts intervene in interpreting Parliament's words? Should the courts go as far as Allan proposes?

Statute law and European law

☐ REVISION NOTE

The interrelationship between statute law and European law is covered in Chapter 2 on European law.

Delegated legislation

KEY DEFINITION: Delegated legislation

Delegated legislation is sometimes referred to as *subordinate* legislation. Check to see which term is used within your course.

Parliament has delegated the power to legislate to various persons and bodies. Hence, **delegated legislation** is a law made by such persons or bodies *with the authority of Parliament.* This authority is granted by an enabling Act (sometimes called a parent Act), which confirms the extent of the authority and any procedural stipulations which are to be followed. The different persons and bodies are as follows:

Person or body	Delegated legislative power
Ministers of the Crown	Statutory instruments (regulations, rules and orders) The procedure for introducing a statutory instrument is usually laid down partly in the enabling (parent) Act and partly in the Statutory Instruments Act 1946. The use of statutory instruments is widespread. In 2003, Parliament passed 45 Acts; almost 3,500 statutory instruments were made in the same period
Local authorities	May make by-laws under the Local Government Act 1972 (but by-laws cannot come into force until affirmed by the appropriate minister)
Semi-public organisations	May also make by-laws under statutory powers (e.g. railway/ transport authorities, the National Trust)
Court rule committees	Make procedural rules for the courts – for example, the Civil Procedure Rule Committee, the Criminal Procedure Rule Committee and the Family Procedure Rule Committee
The Privy Council	May make Orders in Council, such as emergency regulations which have the force of law, or implement resolutions of the United Nations Security Council

Control of delegated legislation by the courts

Unlike Acts of Parliament, delegated legislation may be challenged in the courts via the doctrine of *ultra vires*.

KEY DEFINITION: *Ultra vires*

Ultra vires is a Latin term meaning *beyond (his) powers.*

If you have studied administrative law, you may already be familiar with the concept of *ultra vires* as a potential ground for challenge for **judicial review**; that is, the procedure by which, on the application of an individual, the courts may determine whether a public body has acted lawfully.

If a body acts beyond the powers that are delegated to it, then the delegated legislation can be declared void by the court. This may be procedural (where the delegated legislation was created without following the proper procedure); substantive (where the provisions of the delegated legislation were outside the enabling Act); or where the provisions are irrational (such that no reasonable rule-maker could have arrived at them). Delegated legislation is also *ultra vires* if it conflicts with an earlier Act of Parliament or European legislation (s. 2(4) European Communities Act 1972 – see Chapter 2). You may have covered *Commissioners of Customs & Excise* v. *Cure & Deeley Ltd* [1962] 1 QB 340, DC and *R* v. *Secretary of State for Social Security, ex parte Joint Council for the Welfare of Immigrants* [1997] 1 WLR 275, CA as examples on your course. If not, you may want to look them up now to see how the courts have approached the issue of validity.

Advantages and disadvantages of delegated legislation

Advantages	Disadvantages
Detailed rules and regulations can be implemented relatively quickly	Legislation is not fully debated in Parliament – opportunity for public objection is minimised, less democratic
MPs may not have sufficient knowledge to debate particular specialist areas and may be better served by delegating their authority to those with full knowledge	Delegated legislation is not publicised before and after implementation as widely as Acts of Parliament
There is insufficient Parliamentary time available to debate all Bills in full and delegated legislation enables the most effective use of the limited time available	Proliferation of delegated legislation makes it laborious to keep one's knowledge of it current – it is therefore important to check that your legal research is up to date

■ Statutory interpretation

> Statutory interpretation is a topic that lends itself to both essay *and* problem questions. However, it is also a fundamental building block of legal knowledge, so you should make sure you are as confident with the subject matter as possible.

Why is it needed?

The words of an Act of Parliament are authoritative. The constitutional role of the judiciary is the application of legislation. If the wording of the legislation is ambiguous or unclear, then its meaning will need to be interpreted: while the ordinary meaning of a word in the English language is a matter of *fact*, its legal meaning is, self-evidently, a matter of *law*.

Ambiguity or lack of clarity may arise because the Act has been poorly drafted (using generic or ambiguous terms) or does not cover all eventualities (particularly in relation to complex subject areas). The meanings of words also change over time.

The 'rules' of statutory interpretation

> These 'rules' are sometimes referred to as the *rules of construction*. This is derived from the verb 'to construe' meaning 'to interpret'.

Judges use a variety of different approaches when faced with an issue of statutory interpretation. These are commonly referred to as the 'rules' of interpretation, although they are not strict rules; judges are not bound to follow one (or indeed any) of them and do not have to announce in any way which 'rule' they have used. It is perhaps better, then, to think of them as *approaches* to interpretation or as a framework for discussion, rather than as traditional rules. They are:

- **the literal rule**
- **the golden rule**
- **the mischief rule.**

The literal rule

KEY DEFINITION: Literal rule

> The literal rule provides that words must be given their plain, ordinary and literal meaning.

The rationale behind the use of the literal rule is that if the words of the statute are clear they must be applied as they represent the intention of Parliament as expressed in the words used. This is so *even if the outcome is harsh or undesirable.* This was made clear in the *Sussex Peerage Case* (1844) 1 Cl & Fin 85:

KEY CASE

Sussex Peerage Case (1844) 1 Cl & Fin 85

Concerning: definition of the literal rule

Legal principle

The only rule for construction of Acts of Parliament is that they should be construed according to the intent of the Parliament which passed the Act. If the words . . . are themselves precise and unambiguous, then no more can be necessary than to expound those words in that natural and ordinary sense.

Some examples of its application are as follows:

Case	Comment
Cutter v. *Eagle Star Insurance Co Ltd* [1997] 1 WLR 1082, CA	A car park is not a 'road' for the purposes of the Road Traffic Act 1988. The purpose of a road is a means for cars to move along it to a destination; the purpose of a car park is for cars to stand still. Parking a car on a road does not make it a car park. Driving a car across a car park does not make it a road as it is incidental to its main function.
Whiteley v. *Chappell* (1868) LR 4 QB 147, DC	The defendant had impersonated a dead person and voted in an election in his name. The relevant statute provided that it was an offence to impersonate 'any person entitled to vote' at an election. Since the person impersonated was dead, he was not entitled to vote, and thus Whiteley could not be convicted. Of course, this application of the literal rule ironically went *against* Parliament's intention.

The golden rule

KEY DEFINITION: Golden rule

The golden rule provides that words must be given their plain, ordinary and literal meaning *as far as possible* but only to the extent that they do not produce absurdity (narrow approach) or an affront to public policy (wide approach).

The rationale behind the **golden rule** is that it mitigates some of the potential harshness arising from use of the literal rule. This was referred to in *Grey* v. *Pearson* (1857) 6 HL Cas 61, HL:

KEY CASE

Grey v. *Pearson* (1857) 6 HL Cas 61, HL

Concerning: definition of the golden rule

Legal principle

The grammatical and ordinary sense of the words is to be adhered to unless that would lead to some absurdity, repugnance, or inconsistency with the rest of the instrument, in which case the grammatical and ordinary sense of the words may be modified so as to avoid that absurdity and inconsistency, but not farther.

Some examples of its application are as follows:

Case	Comment
R v. *Allen* (1872) LR 1 CCR 367 (narrow approach; absurdity)	Section 57 of the Offences against the Person Act 1861 provided that 'whosoever being married shall marry any other person during the lifetime of his spouse' shall commit bigamy. If 'marry' had been interpreted literally, the offence could never have been committed, since no one married could ever marry another. The words 'shall marry' were interpreted as 'shall go through the ceremony of marriage'.
Re Sigsworth [1935] Ch 89, DC (wide approach; affront to public policy)	Under the Administration of Estates Act 1925 the estate of a person dying intestate (i.e. without leaving a will) was to be divided among the 'issue'. Mrs Sigsworth was murdered by her son who stood to inherit her estate. Even though there was only one possible interpretation of the word 'issue', the court held that the son could not inherit the estate as it would be contrary to the public-policy principle that a murderer should not benefit from his crime; the golden rule was applied in preference to the literal rule.

The mischief rule

KEY DEFINITION: Mischief rule

The mischief rule (or the rule in *Heydon's Case* (1584) 3 Co Rep 7a) involves an examination of the *former* law in an attempt to deduce Parliament's intention ('mischief' here means 'wrong' or 'harm'). There are four points to consider:

1 What was the common law before the making of the Act?
2 What was the mischief and defect for which the common law did not provide?
3 What was the remedy proposed by Parliament to rectify the situation?
4 What was the true reason for that remedy?

The rule was restated in *Jones* v. *Wrotham Park Settled Estates* [1980] AC 74, HL in terms of three conditions:

1 It must be possible to determine precisely the mischief that the Act was intended to remedy.
2 It must be apparent that Parliament had failed to deal with the mischief.
3 It must be possible to state the additional words that would have been inserted had the omission been drawn to Parliament's attention.

Some examples of its application are as follows:

Case	Comment
Corkery v. *Carpenter* [1951] 1 KB 102, DC	Section 12 of the Licensing Act 1872 provided that a person drunk in charge of a 'carriage' on the highway could be arrested without a warrant. The defendant was found drunk in charge of a bicycle. Although it could be argued that a bicycle is not a carriage in the normal meaning of the word, the Divisional Court held that a bicycle *was* a carriage for the purposes of the Act; the mischief here was prevention of drunken persons on the highway in charge of some form of transportation for the purposes of public order and safety.
Manchester City Council v. *McCann* [1999] QB 1214, CA	Section 118(1)(a) of the County Courts Act 1984 provides that county courts may deal with anyone who 'wilfully insults the judge . . . or any juror or witness, or any officer of the court'. The court held that a threat was an insult for the purposes of the Act; the mischief here was protection of various participants in the civil process. Even though a threat is not necessarily an insult using normal meanings, the ability for the court to deal with insults but not threats was contrary to Parliament's intention.

Rules of language

In addition to the rules of construction, there are also rules of language which the courts may apply. They are:

- *ejusdem generis*
- *noscitur a sociis*
- *expressio unius est exclusio alterius.*

Ejusdem generis

KEY DEFINITION: *Ejusdem generis*

Ejusdem generis means 'of the same type'. In other words, if a word with general meaning follows a list of specific words, then the general word only applies to things of the same type as the specific words.

Think about the following situations:

Situation	Comment
Does a 'house, office, room or other place' include an outdoor betting ring?	Since the specific places are all indoors, an outdoor betting ring is not included. *Powell* v. *Kempton Park Racecourse* [1899] AC 143, HL
Is a piece of (accidentally broken) glass covered by 'any gun, pistol, hangar, cutlass, bludgeon or other offensive weapon'?	The list contains items made or adapted for the purposes of causing harm, so a piece of accidentally broken glass is not included. *Wood* v. *Commissioner of Police of the Metropolis* [1986] 1 WLR 796, DC

Noscitur a sociis

KEY DEFINITION: *Noscitur a sociis*

Noscitur a sociis means that a word is 'known by the company it keeps'.

Words in a statute derive meaning from the words surrounding them. There is a presumption that words in a list have related meanings and are to be interpreted in relation to each other. For example, in *Pengelly* v. *Bell Punch Co Ltd* [1964] 1 WLR 1055, CA, the court held that 'floors' in a statute requiring 'floors, steps, stairs, passages and gangways' to be clear did not cover part of a floor used for storage. The other words in the list all related to passageways.

Expressio unius est exclusio alterius

> **KEY DEFINITION:** *Expressio unius est exclusio alterius*
>
> *Expressio unius est exclusio alterius* means that to 'express one thing is to exclude others'; in other words, to list a number of specific things may be interpreted as impliedly excluding others of the same type.

Case	Comment
R v. *Inhabitants of Sedgley* (1831) 2 B & Ald 65	The poor rate levied on owners of 'lands, houses, tithes and coal mines' could not be levied on owners of limestone mines, as these were impliedly excluded by the specific mention of *coal* mines.

Presumptions

In addition to the rules of construction and rules of language, there are also a number of presumptions which are made when interpreting legislation. The most important of these are as follows:

Presumption	Comment
Against alteration of the common law	Although Parliament can change the existing common law, such an intention cannot be *implied* (e.g. *Beswick* v. *Beswick* [1968] AC 58, HL)
Against retrospective operation of statute	It is presumed that statutes do not operate retrospectively (this is particularly important in Acts which criminalise, since it could lead to criminal liability arising for acts which were lawful at the time they were committed). This presumption, however, can be rebutted by express words by Parliament (e.g. Police (Detention and Bail) Act 2011; War Crimes Act 1991; War Damage Act 1965 overruling the House of Lords decision in *Burmah Oil Co Ltd* v. *Lord Advocate* [1965] AC 75, HL)

▶

Presumption	Comment
Against deprivation of liberty	Parliament is presumed not to intend to deprive a person of his liberty; if it does, clear words must be used and will be construed so as to interfere with the subject's liberty as little as possible (e.g. *R (on the application of H)* v. *Mental Health Review Tribunal for North and East London Region* [2002] QB 1, CA)
Against deprivation of property and against interference with private rights	Parliament is presumed not to wish to interfere with a person's private rights or deprive him of his property (without compensation) (e.g. *Glassbrook Bros* v. *Leyson* [1933] 2 KB 91, CA; *Bowles* v. *Bank of England* [1913] 1 Ch 57, DC)
Against binding the Crown	Parliament is presumed not to bind the Crown except expressly or by necessary implication of the statute (e.g. Equal Pay Act 1970; Sex Discrimination Act 1975)
Against ousting the jurisdiction of the courts	Even where clear ouster clauses have been used, the courts will try to construe them in a way which permits judicial review (e.g. *Anisminic Ltd* v. *Foreign Compensation Commission* [1969] 2 AC 147, CA)
Against criminal liability without *mens rea* (a guilty mind)	There is a presumption that, for statutory criminal offences, Parliament intended no liability without proof of *mens rea* (e.g. *R* v. *K (Age of Consent: Reasonable Belief)* [2002] 1 AC 462, HL). This can be rebutted by express words or by implication in offences of *strict liability* (such as speeding)

Intrinsic aids to interpretation

Any statute must be read as a whole. That is to say that before looking outside the statute to seek its meaning, every word within the statute should be considered in the search for meaning. There are a number of areas within the statute which could potentially be used as an intrinsic aid to construction.

Statutory component	Comment
Short title	This is usually descriptive only and therefore of limited value
Long title	The long title may be considered but only where there is ambiguity within the body of the Act (e.g. *R (on the application of Quintavalle)* v. *Secretary of State for Health* [2003] 2 AC 687, HL)

Statutory component	Comment
Preamble	Preambles tend not to be found in recent statutes. Where preambles do exist, they may be considered for guidance purposes in cases of ambiguity
Side notes	These are not debated in Parliament and are not normally used in determining the precise scope of a provision (*DPP* v. *Schildkamp* [1971] AC 1, HL); however, they can give some general indication of the provision's purpose (*DPP* v. *Johnson* [1995] 1 WLR 728, DC)
Punctuation	Old statutes did not use punctuation at all. Punctuation may be used as an aid to interpretation where there is ambiguity (*DPP* v. *Schildkamp*, HL)
Examples	Statutes may provide examples to illustrate how the Act might work or how terminology within it might be used. These are part of the statute and carry great persuasive authority (examples include s. 44(6) Criminal Justice Act 2003; Consumer Credit Act 1974; Law of Property Act 1925)
Schedules	Statutes may contain schedules which include an interpretation and definition section (e.g. Schedule 1, Interpretation Act 1978). These are strongly persuasive

Extrinsic aids to interpretation

Extrinsic aids to interpretation are those found outside the statute itself. The Interpretation Act 1978 defines words that are commonly used within legislation (for example: in any Act, unless the contrary intention appears, words importing the masculine gender include the feminine and *vice versa*; 'land' includes buildings and other structures, land covered with water, and any estate, interest, easement, servitude or right in or over land). Where a word has no specific legal meaning, dictionaries may also be used. Courts may also look at earlier or related statutes. Historically, since the court was only allowed to interpret the words used, reference to preparatory works (*travaux préparatoires*) was not permitted. This meant that courts could not refer to records of Parliamentary debate on the statute in *Hansard*. However, this rule was relaxed in the early 1990s following the ruling of the House of Lords in *Pepper* v. *Hart*.

KEY CASE

Pepper v. *Hart* **[1993] AC 593, HL**

Concerning: statutory interpretation; reference to Hansard

Legal principle

The House of Lords held that the rule against the use of Hansard as an extrinsic aid to interpretation would be relaxed to permit reference to parliamentary materials where:

(a) the legislation is ambiguous or obscure, or its literal meaning leads to an absurdity;

(b) the material relied on consists of statements by a minister or other promoter of the Bill (*Wilson* v. *First County Trust Ltd (No. 2)* [2004] 1 AC 816, HL); and

(c) the statements relied on are clear.

✎ EXAM TIP

A common mistake when discussing *Pepper* v. *Hart* is to say that it permits courts to refer to *Hansard*. Remember that the rule only applies in the situation where there is an ambiguity or absurdity and there are clear statements made by the promoter of the Bill (usually a minister). The conditions attached to the rule in *Pepper* v. *Hart* are often overlooked.

✎ EXAM TIP

If a problem question on statutory interpretation refers to things said in debates, this is usually a signpost that some discussion of *Pepper* v. *Hart* will be required.

The purposive approach

The purposive approach involves seeking an interpretation of the law which gives effect to its general purpose. It is based upon the mischief rule. It allows the courts to look beyond the words used in the provision to find an interpretation which furthers its general purpose. It is now regarded as the predominant approach to statutory interpretation in the United Kingdom. In *R (on the application of Quintavalle)* v. *Secretary of State for Health* [2003] 2 AC 687, HL, Lord Steyn commented that 'the pendulum has swung towards purposive methods of construction'.

The teleological approach

The **teleological approach** requires that not just the purpose but also the spirit of the legislation is considered. It is therefore much broader than the purposive approach. It is particularly important when considering European law which is often drafted in terms of wide general principles and not in the detailed manner employed in domestic legislation.

Section 2(4) of the European Communities Act 1972 provides that the courts should give preference to an interpretation which gives effect to the general spirit of the legislation. This means that the courts often have to consider questions of wide economic or social policy. In some circumstances this involves the courts reading certain words into legislation; this is a clear departure from using the literal words as chosen by Parliament. For instance in both *Pickstone* v. *Freemans plc* [1989] AC 66, HL and *Litster* v. *Forth Dry Dock and Engineering Co. Ltd* [1990] 1 AC 546, HL, words were read into the legislation by necessary implication to give effect to the United Kingdom's obligations under Community law.

✎ EXAM TIP

Always remember to consider using the purposive/teleological approach in problem questions on interpretation. In other words, construct an argument around your view of what a particular piece of legislation set out to achieve and whether that aim is met by application of any of the other rules of construction. With any problem you should be methodical.

Remember to consider all rules of construction, even if it is simply to discount them. If you do decide that a particular rule is inappropriate, say why – otherwise the examiner will have no evidence that you even knew of its existence and you will gain no credit for knowing it.

■ Putting it all together

Answer guidelines

See the sample question at the start of the chapter. A diagram illustrating how to structure your answer is available on the companion website.

Approaching the question

This is a typical essay question on the 'rules' of statutory interpretation. Analysing the quotation in the question reveals that you are required to consider a number of key

▶

issues: a discussion of three 'so-called rules of statutory interpretation': in other words, the literal, golden and mischief rules.

Important points to include

Your answer should certainly engage with the main issues raised by the quotation:

- an analysis of why it is 'misleading' to call them rules; leading to:
- why it is better to consider them as general approaches.

However, this is not all that is needed. The question asks for a discussion of the above points 'in relation to the role of the judiciary'. You should therefore consider including points such as:

- why legislation needs interpretation;
- the role of the judiciary in its interpretation;
- the role of the judiciary in relation to the role of Parliament;
- do judges make law?
- *should* judges make law?

 Make your answer stand out

- Relate your description back to the quotation provided.
- Give an example of each of the rules from case law.
- Consider the deeper questions – such as whether the involvement of the judiciary encroaches on Parliamentary sovereignty? Include some discussion on how case law can set binding precedent (see Chapter 4) and that judges, therefore, can make law by interpretation. To what extent should they be able to do this without 'overstepping the mark' set in the express words of Parliament? Remember that Parliament is supposed to be the supreme legislative body.
- Comment on how none of the approaches is binding, and how this can potentially lead to a wide variety of possible outcomes – use case examples to illustrate.

READ TO IMPRESS

Allan, T.R.S. (1985) 'The limits of parliamentary sovereignty', *Public Law* 614.

Bates, T. (1995) 'The contemporary use of legislative history in the United Kingdom', 54 *Cambridge Law Journal* 127.

Bennion, F. (2002) *Statutory Interpretation*, 4th edn, London: Butterworths.

Dicey, A.V. (1982) *The Law of the Constitution*, 10th edn, Indianapolis: Liberty Fund.

Friedman, L. (1988) 'On interpretation of laws', 11 *Ratio Juris* 252.

Jenkins, C. (1999) 'Helping the reader of Bills and Acts', 149 *New Law Journal* 798.

www.pearsoned.co.uk/lawexpress

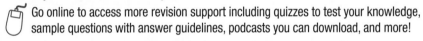 Go online to access more revision support including quizzes to test your knowledge, sample questions with answer guidelines, podcasts you can download, and more!

European law

2

Revision checklist

Essential points you should know:

☐ The main European institutions and their functions

☐ The main provisions of the European Communities Act 1972

☐ The main primary and secondary sources of European law

☐ The meaning of the terms *direct applicability* and *direct effect* (both *horizontal* and *vertical*)

☐ The extent to which European law is supreme over domestic law

■ Topic map

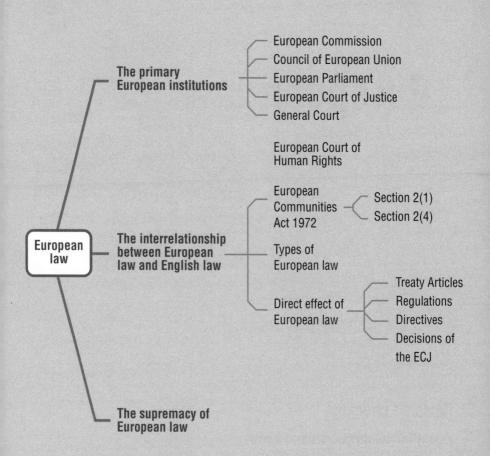

▊ Introduction

European law plays an increasingly influential role in the English legal system

The UK became a member of the European Economic Community (the EEC) on 1 January 1973. However, since international law is not recognised as part of the English legal system unless it is incorporated into English law by statute, the United Kingdom's Community obligations had to be fulfilled via the enactment of the European Communities Act 1972. Although a large part of our national law remains unaffected, certain high-profile areas are significantly affected; these include employment law, commercial and consumer law, environmental law and law relating to the free movement of goods and workers throughout Europe. Since the European Communities Act 1972 has effectively incorporated European legislation into domestic law, it is important to understand the circumstances in which European law will have a bearing on English law as it is a topic which could be combined with a wide range of other more 'traditional' question types. Since European law covers a large range of topics, this chapter will concentrate on the aspects of European law as far as the impact upon the *operation* of the English legal system; your European law exam will cover the *substance* of European law.

ASSESSMENT ADVICE

Within the context of an English Legal system course, it is still possible to encounter both essay and problem questions which concern the operation or impact of European law.

Essay questions

Typically take one of two approaches, either requiring a discussion of the impact that European law has had on the English legal system, or as part of a more general question on sources of law, of which European law forms one part (along with domestic legislation and law made through judicial interpretation or the operation of the doctrine of precedent).

Problem questions

Typically take the form of a series of pieces of (often fictitious) European legislation which are potentially relevant to a problem scenario. You are then asked to analyse whether or not they apply, and if so, why and with what effect. This may be combined with other matters of statutory interpretation or precedent. In a question like this, a detailed understanding of horizontal and vertical direct effect is essential.

Sample question

Could you answer this question? Below is a typical problem question that could arise on this topic. Guidelines on answering the question are included at the end of the chapter, whilst a sample essay question and guidance on tackling it can be found on the companion website.

PROBLEM QUESTION

Dave is a mental health nurse working in the NHS; his wife, Kate, works doing the same job in a private nursing home. A recent European Directive stated that all member states must ensure that all mental healthcare professionals receive a minimum 5% pay rise each year. The deadline for implementation of the Directive was May 2009. It is now June 2012 and neither Dave nor Kate has received any pay rise at all.

Advise Dave and Kate of their rights under European law (if any).

The primary European institutions

It is important to be able to distinguish between the different institutions established by the EC Treaty and to understand their functions.

Institution	Established by	Function
European Commission	Articles 211–219 EC	Formulates policies which are consistent with the various Treaties of the European Union (e.g. the EC Treaty and the Treaty on European Union). Members are politicians appointed by the member states.
Council of the European Union (also known as the Council of Ministers)	Article 202 EC	Main law-making body of the Community. Membership fluctuates depending on the subject matter of the debate.
European Parliament	Articles 182–201 EC	Originated as a discussion chamber, but is becoming part of the legislative process. The Commission and Council may consult the Parliament. In exceptional circumstances the Parliament can veto legislation.

Institution	Established by	Function
Court of Justice of the European Communities (commonly 'European Court of Justice', 'ECJ' or 'CJEC')	Articles 220–244 EC	Comprises one judge from each member state and eight Advocates-General. Hears appeals on points of law from Court of First Instance. Sits in Luxembourg.
General Court (Formerly Court of First Instance)	Article 225 EC	Comprises judges appointed by the member states. As its former name suggests, hears a wide variety of European cases at **first instance**.
European Council	Not established by the EC Treaty	Comprises the Heads of State or Government of the EU member states.

We shall now look at the jurisdiction of the European Court of Justice and General Court in a little more detail.

! Don't be tempted to . . .

It is vitally important not to confuse the European Court of Justice (which sits in Luxembourg) with the European Court of Human Rights (which sits in Strasbourg).

It is also important not to confuse the Council of the European Union with the Council of Europe. The Council of Europe is a separate body and has responsibility for the European Court of Human Rights.

📖 REVISION NOTE

When considering the jurisdiction of the European Court of Justice and General Court, you may wish to skip forward to Chapter 3 and revisit the domestic institutions of the court system.

European Court of Justice

Jurisdiction	The European Court of Justice (ECJ/CJEC) primarily:
	■ Gives **'preliminary rulings'**. National courts may make interim references directly to the ECJ if they need clarification on how a particular piece of European legislation should be interpreted. The need for such references will arise during the course of a domestic action, typically in the House of Lords. In other words, if a court cannot make a ruling because it is unsure how to construe a piece of European legislation, then it can effectively suspend the proceedings before it to ask the ECJ for its opinion. These are made under Article 234 EC, so you will often hear them referred to as **'Article 234 references'**.
	■ Hears actions against member states for failure to meet Treaty obligations. These actions may be brought by the European Commission (Article 226 EC) or by one member state against another (Article 227 EC). ECJ may impose fines as a result (Article 228 EC).
Personnel	■ Judges appointed by agreement among the member states.
	■ One judge per state.
	■ Assisted by Advocates-General.

General Court

Jurisdiction	The Court of First Instance (CFI) was set up by the Single European Act 1986 in an attempt to cope with the increasing caseload of the ECJ. As its name suggests, it hears a wide variety of European cases at first instance brought by individuals rather than by member states. There is a right to appeal to the ECJ on matters of law. It became known as the General Court (EGC) from 1 December 2010.
Personnel	Judges appointed by agreement among the member states. At least one judge per state.

European Court of Human Rights

The European Court of Human Rights is *not* an EU institution. However, because of its pan-European dimension and influence, its jurisdiction and personnel are included here for completeness.

Jurisdiction	The European Court of Human Rights:
	Hears actions from individuals relating to alleged breaches of the European Convention on Human Rights.
Personnel	Judges from each state that is a party to the European Convention on Human Rights (1950).

The interrelationship between European law and English law

The European Communities Act 1972

The most important provision relating to European law is s. 2(1) of the European Communities Act 1972.

KEY STATUTE

Section 2(1) of the European Communities Act 1972

All such rights, powers, liabilities, obligations and restrictions from time to time created or arising by or under the Treaties, and all such remedies and procedures from time to time provided for by or under the Treaties, as in accordance with the Treaties are without further enactment to be given legal effect or used in the United Kingdom shall be recognised and available in law, and be enforced, allowed and followed accordingly.

This means that European law, irrespective of whether it arises from treaties or Community regulations and whether it has already been made or is to be made in the future is directly applicable in the United Kingdom. Moreover, s. 2(4) of the Act provides that any 'enactment' passed or to be passed in the United Kingdom must be interpreted with applicable European law in mind.

KEY STATUTE

Section 2(4) of the European Communities Act 1972

Any enactment passed or to be passed . . . shall be construed and have effect subject to the foregoing provisions of this section.

Before moving on to discuss the enforceability of European law, it is necessary to tackle some potentially confusing terminology.

> **KEY DEFINITIONS: Directly applicable and directly effective**
>
> A provision of European law will be *directly applicable* if it automatically becomes part of the law of a member state without the need for the member state to enact any legislation itself.
>
> A provision of European law will be *directly effective* if (and only if) it creates rights which individuals may rely upon in their national courts and are enforceable by those courts.
>
> Thus, *direct applicability* is concerned with the incorporation of European law into the legal system of a member state, whereas *direct effect* is concerned with its *enforceability*.

Whether any particular piece of European legislation will be **directly applicable** or **directly effective** will firstly depend on its type.

Types of European law

Primary	Secondary
Treaty of Rome 1957	Regulations
Single European Act 1985	Directives
Maastricht Treaty 1992	Decisions issued by the Commission
Treaty of Amsterdam 1996	
Treaty of Nice 2001	
Treaty of Lisbon 2009	

The various Treaties listed in the table reflect many of the stages in the evolution of European law. As the EU expanded to include more member states, a new European Constitution was proposed which contained significant reforms to both the institutions of the EU and its operation. This proposed constitution was rejected by France and the Netherlands. Following this rejection, a new Reform Treaty was drawn up and was signed in Lisbon on 13 December 2007. It was originally intended to have been ratified by all member states by the end of 2008. However, a referendum on the Treaty resulted in its rejection by the Irish electorate in 2008. This decision was reversed in a second referendum in 2009.

The Treaty of Lisbon was ratified by the UK on 19 June 2008 by the European Union (Amendment) Act 2008 and came into force on 1 December 2009.

The Treaty of Lisbon amended the Treaty on European Union and the Treaty Establishing the European Community (which was also renamed the Treaty on the Functioning of the European Union). Its most significant changes included:

- the creation of a long-term President of the European Council;

- the elimination of the pillar system;

- more qualified majority voting in the Council of Ministers;

- increased involvement of the European Parliament in the legislative process;

- the Charter of Fundamental Rights being given the status of a legally binding instrument.

Direct effect of European law

Before examining which of the different types of European legislation have direct effect (that is, can be relied upon by individuals in national courts and be enforced by those courts) it is necessary to understand the distinction between *vertical* **direct effect** and *horizontal* **direct effect** (see Figure 2.1). If a provision is not directly effective it may not be relied upon by an individual.

Figure 2.1

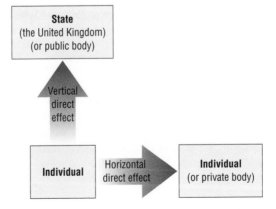

KEY DEFINITIONS: Vertical and horizontal direct effect

A provision of European law has *vertical* direct effect if it is enforceable against a member state in its own courts. In the United Kingdom this means that vertically directly effective provisions can be enforced against the United Kingdom itself, as well as against local authorities, health authorities (*Marshall* v. *Southampton and South West Hampshire Area Health Authority (No. 2)* [1994] QB 126, CJEC) and nationalised industries (*Foster* v. *British Gas plc* [1991] 1 QB 405, CJEC).

A provision of European law has *horizontal* direct effect if it can be enforced against another individual.

Treaty Articles

All Treaty Articles have vertical direct effect following the case of *Van Gend en Loos* v. *Nederlandse Administratie der Belastingen*.

KEY CASE

Van Gend en Loos v. *Nederlandse Administratie der Belastingen* **[1963] ECR 1, CJEC**

Concerning: vertical direct effect of Treaty Articles

Facts

A Dutch company wanted to enforce Article 12 EEC against the Dutch customs authorities which had increased the duty on imports. The matter was referred to the European Court of Justice.

Legal principle

The Treaty Article created individual enforceable rights against the state (i.e. it had vertical direct effect) because its terms were ' clear, precise and unconditional ' and there was no room for discretion in implementation. Its implementation required no further legislation in member states (i.e. it was *directly applicable*). Therefore, member states had no discretion in the means of its implementation. These criteria are often referred to simply as the *Van Gend* criteria.

Treaty Articles may also have horizontal direct effect (*Defrenne* v. *Sabena (No. 2)* [1976] ECR 455, CJEC).

Therefore, Treaty Articles can be enforced directly in UK courts, regardless of any other domestic legislation.

Regulations

Article 249 EC states that a Regulation shall 'have general application' and shall be 'binding in its entirety and directly applicable in all member states'. Therefore, subject to satisfying the *Van Gend* criteria, Regulations, like Treaty Articles, have both vertical (*Leonesio* v. *Italian Ministry of Agriculture* Case 93/71 [1972] ECR 287, CJEC) and horizontal (*Antonio Munoz Cia SA* v. *Frumar Ltd* Case C-253/00 [2002] ECR-I/7289, CJEC) direct effect.

Directives

Article 249 EC demonstrates that Directives are fundamentally different from Regulations. Directives are 'binding as to the result to be achieved, upon each member state to which it is addressed, but shall leave to the national authority the choice of form and methods'. In other words, Directives tell the member states what needs to be done, but leave the states to decide what provisions of domestic law to enact in order to implement that Directive. There is usually a specified period of time for the member states to implement any given Directive. Therefore:

- Directives are not directly applicable;

- Directives do not have horizontal direct effect;

- however, Directives *may* have vertical direct effect if:

  □ they satisfy the *Van Gend* criteria; *and*

  □ the time for implementation has passed (*Pubblico Ministero* v. *Ratti* Case 148/78 [1979] ECR 1629, CJEC).

Finally, a member state which has failed to implement a Directive may be liable to compensate individuals who have suffered as a result (*Francovich* v. *Italian Republic* [1991] ECR I-4845, CJEC). In other words, if an individual has lost out because of defective implementation of a Directive, they may be able to 'sue the state' for the loss.

! Don't be tempted to . . .

Although Articles, Regulations and Directives are all items of European law, they are often confused. Treaty Articles are the basic principles upon which European law is founded. These set out a broad framework and establish the fundamental legal concepts, often in very general terms. The Articles are supplemented by Regulations which provide the next level of detail – however, since Regulations are immediately directly applicable, then by virtue of s. 2(1) of the European Communities Act 1972 they do not require any further legislative work for their implementation. Directives often provide the real detail on a given area; here it is recognised that individual member states may need to implement ▶

them in slightly different ways, to reflect their own national cultures or customs. Therefore, as long as the objective of the Directive is met, each state is given discretion as to how it is implemented in its domestic law. Many pieces of important and influential UK legislation have arisen from the implementation of European Directives, such as the Equal Pay Act 1970 and the Sex Discrimination Act 1975.

Decisions of the ECJ

Article 249 EC provides that a decision of the ECJ is 'binding in its entirety upon those to whom it is addressed, who may be either individuals or member states'. Thus they are not directly applicable, but are capable of having direct effect.

✎ EXAM TIP

It is important to remember the *Van Gend* criteria when talking about Regulations and Directives as well as Treaty Articles.

You might find Figure 2.2 useful when thinking about the horizontal and vertical direct effect of Treaty Articles, Regulations and Directives.

Figure 2.2

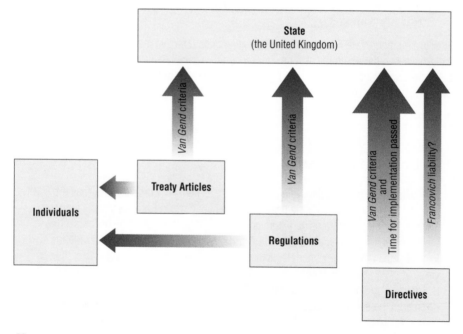

Figure 2.3

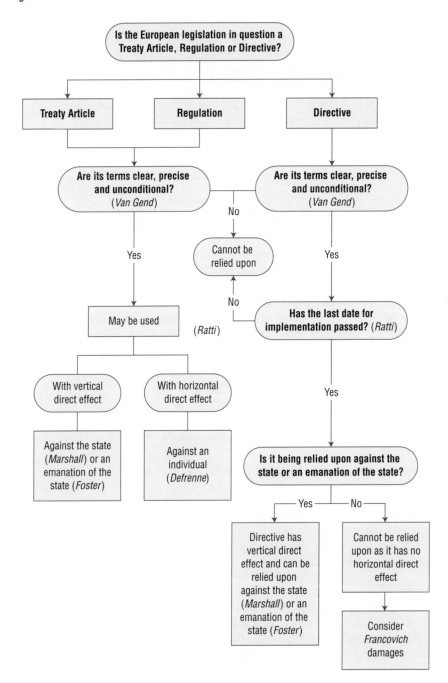

! Don't be tempted to . . .

The different ways in which different pieces of European legislation can apply to a given set of facts can be confusing. When looking at a problem question, it is best to take a methodical and structured approach, such as that set out in Figure 2.3. A particular twist that examiners sometimes use would be to ask you to consider the application of, say, a Treaty Article and then follow it up by asking if your answer would be any different if the legislation in question was a Regulation or Directive. Remember the criteria for vertical and horizontal direct effect and the complication that the latest implementation date for a Directive must also have passed.

■ The supremacy of European law

From the point of view of the Community, where there is a conflict between European law and the law of member states, European law prevails. This has been clear since *van Gend en Loos* where the ECJ stated that 'the Community constitutes a new legal order . . . for whose benefit the states have limited their sovereign rights'. In other words, the Community's view is that the autonomy of the member states to act as they wish has been limited by virtue of their membership of the Community. Does this mean that the enactment of the European Communities Act 1972 prevents Parliament from introducing new statutes which conflict with European law? This was put to the test in the *Factortame* cases.

KEY CASE

R v. Secretary of State for Transport, ex parte Factortame Ltd (No. 2) [1990] 2 AC 85, HL

Concerning: supremacy of European law in the United Kingdom

Facts

A conflict arose between provisions of the EC Treaty preventing discrimination on the grounds of nationality and Part II of the Merchant Shipping Act 1988 which provided that UK-registered fishing boats fishing for UK quotas (allocated by the EC) must be owned and managed by UK citizens.

Legal principle

The House of Lords upheld an ECJ opinion that it could grant an interim injunction against the Crown to prevent it enforcing an Act which contravened European law; an act that was previously constitutionally impossible. The House of Lords later held that parts of the Merchant Shipping Act were incompatible with the EC Treaty. This situation was reconciled by Lord Bridge who considered a fictional 'invisible clause' – since s. 2(4) of the European Communities Act 1972 states that any enactment must have regard to Community obligations, this effectively meant that Parliament's intention was that all future legislation would be compliant with the United Kingdom's community obligations and would contain an invisible clause to this effect – unless the incompatibility was very important, in which case it could be explicitly excluded in the new legislation. Lord Bridge stated that:

> Whatever limitation of its sovereignty Parliament accepted when it enacted the European Communities Act 1972 it was entirely voluntary . . . when decisions of the Court of Justice have exposed areas of United Kingdom law which failed to implement Council Directives, Parliament has always loyally accepted the obligation to make appropriate and prompt amendments. Thus there is nothing in any way novel in according supremacy to rules of Community law.

In doing so, the House of Lords affirmed that, for all future cases, where a statute is silent on a matter covered by European law, it is presumed that it is intended to comply with European law.

■ Putting it all together

Answer guidelines

See the sample question at the start of the chapter. A diagram illustrating how to structure your answer is available on the companion website.

Approaching the question

This question involves the application of a European Directive. It is important to be methodical when tackling questions like this. One way in which you could do this would be to work through the flowchart in Figure 2.3 and apply the law to the facts of this particular question.

Important points to include

- Remember the criteria for a Directive to have direct effect:
    - □ its terms must be 'clear, precise and unconditional' and there must be no room for discretion in implementation (the *Van Gend* criteria);
    - □ the deadline for implementation must have passed (*Ratti*). ▶

- The deadline has passed, so if the wording of the Directive satisfies the *Van Gend* criteria then it will have direct effect.

- Directives only have vertical direct effect – this means they may be enforced against the state or emanations of the state (*Foster*) but not against private entities.

- Dave works for the NHS; since this is a state body (*Marshall*), he may rely directly on the Directive against his employer.

- Kate works for a private employer; this is not the state or an emanation of the state, therefore Kate may not rely upon the Directive; it does not have horizontal direct effect.

- However, Kate may be able to rely on the principle from *Francovich* to 'sue' the state for her losses as a result of its failure to implement the Directive.

 Make your answer stand out

- Make sure you state the *Van Gend* criteria accurately.

- Be clear why it is important for the date for implementation of the Directive to have passed.

- Use the terms *vertical* and *horizontal* direct effect accurately – it is important to be precise to distinguish your answer from that of a student with a more superficial knowledge of the subject area.

- Comment on the possibility of *Francovich* damages; this is often overlooked in questions involving reliance on Directives.

READ TO IMPRESS

Craig, P. and G. de Burca (2011) *EU Law: Text, Cases and Materials*, 5th edn, Oxford: OUP.

Fairhurst, J. (2010) *Law of the European Union*, 8th edn, Harlow: Longman.

Weatherill, S. (2010) *Cases and Materials on EU Law*, 9th edn, Oxford: OUP.

www.pearsoned.co.uk/lawexpress

 Go online to access more revision support including quizzes to test your knowledge, sample questions with answer guidelines, podcasts you can download, and more!

The institutions

3

■ Topic map

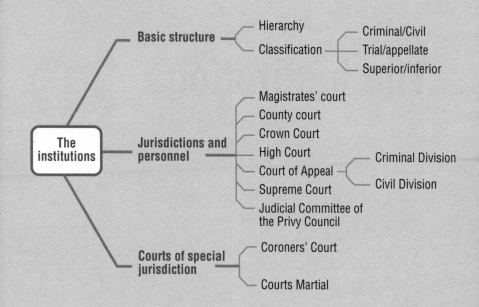

■ Introduction

Without a set of institutions to enforce legal rules, there would be no legal system

A set of rules cannot exist usefully in isolation. There needs to be a system of courts to hear cases at first instance, as well as higher courts which offer the mechanism for individuals to bring appeals arising from the outcome of cases in lower courts. The system of criminal and civil appeals will be dealt with in Chapters 6 and 7 respectively. Furthermore, as you will see when looking at the doctrine of judicial precedent in Chapter 4, there are rules which determine whether or not a particular court will be bound by a decision of a higher court – generally meaning that it will have to follow the particular legal reasoning of that higher court. You should see, then, that a thorough understanding of the institutions of the modern court system is vital to your study of law. Without knowing the hierarchy of the courts, for instance, you would not be able to understand whether any particular judgment might be binding on another court, or follow the route that a particular civil or criminal case might take on appeal.

ASSESSMENT ADVICE

It would be unusual for an exam question to require only knowledge of the institutions. However, it is very common for questions including judicial precedent or the civil or criminal appeals process to begin by requiring you to describe the hierarchy of the courts in some way. The order in which you do this and the information which you select to write about each court will depend on the overall context of the question. It is very important therefore to ensure that you have a thorough understanding of the institutions and their hierarchy so that you can be prepared to answer such questions effectively.

■ Sample question

Could you answer this question? Below is a typical essay question that could arise on this topic. Guidelines on answering the question are included at the end of the chapter, whilst a sample problem question and guidance on tackling it can be found on the companion website.

ESSAY QUESTION

Outline the structure of the court system in England and Wales and describe how this structure relates to the appeals process for civil and criminal cases.

■ The basic structure of the court system

Hierarchy

In addition to the main institutions shown in Figure 3.1 (on page 45), there are also some additional courts with special jurisdiction such as Coroners' Courts and Courts Martial which will be dealt with at the end of this chapter. As you will see later in this chapter, the distinction between the criminal and civil jurisdictions of the courts is not always clear-cut.

📖 **REVISION NOTE**

For completeness, the diagram shows those institutions which are outside the institutions of the English legal system but nevertheless have a bearing on the way it operates. The European Court of Justice and General Court are dealt with in Chapter 2 on European law.

✎ **EXAM TIP**

When discussing *magistrates'* courts or *Coroners'* Courts, don't forget the possessive apostrophe after 'magistrates' or 'Coroners'. Remember also that 'magistrates' court' has a small 'm' and 'county court' has a small 'c', whereas other courts (such as the High Court and Crown Court) have initial capitals. This might sound trivial, but markers will warm to answers which are written correctly. Language is the only tool that a lawyer has and it is essential that you use it properly.

Classification of the courts

Courts can be classified in a number of ways:

- criminal and civil courts
- trial and appellate courts
- superior and inferior courts.

Criminal and civil courts

Criminal courts	Civil courts
Decide guilt or innocence according to the parameters of the criminal law and dispense punishment to convicted offenders	Primarily deal with the resolution of disputes between individuals and award appropriate remedies (usually damages – money paid in compensation) to the injured party

Figure 3.1

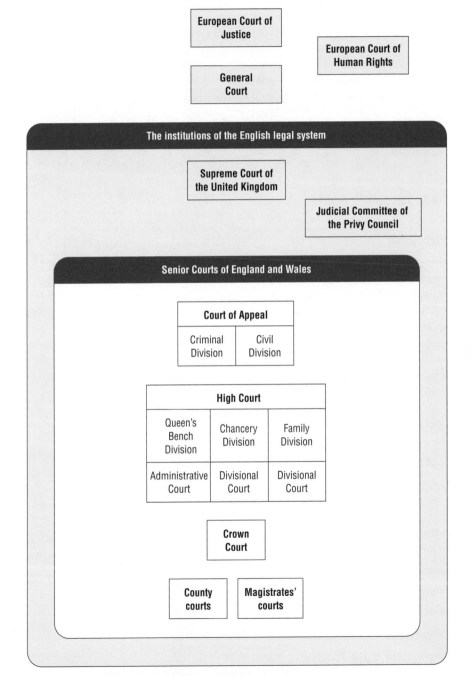

! Don't be tempted to . . .

A particular set of facts can give rise to proceedings in both the criminal and civil courts. For instance, if you were knocked down and injured by a reckless driver while walking down the street, this could lead to a case in the criminal courts (for a possible breach of the Road Traffic Acts) and in the civil courts (to seek compensation in the tort of negligence for your injuries).

The Crown Court deals almost exclusively with criminal matters. The county court has only civil jurisdiction. However, all the other courts have both criminal and civil jurisdictions.

Trial and appellate courts

Trial courts	Appellate courts
Hear cases 'at first instance' (the first time a case is heard in court – before any appeals). Consider the matters of fact and law in the case and make an appropriate ruling	Consider the application of legal principles to a case that has already been heard at first instance. Some appellate courts also have jurisdiction to reconsider disputed issues of fact

Trial and appellate functions are often combined within one court, as you will see when considering the functions of each court in more detail.

Superior and inferior courts

Superior courts	Inferior courts
Unlimited geographic and financial jurisdiction – generally hear the more important and/or difficult cases with no restrictions of area or sums of money involved	Limited geographic and/or financial jurisdiction – generally deal with more straightforward cases
Supreme Court	**county courts**
Court of Appeal	magistrates' courts
High Court	**Coroners' Courts**
Crown Court	**Courts Martial**
Employment Appeal Tribunal	

The courts that are shown in **bold** in the table are also *courts of record*. This means that records of their proceedings are kept at the Public Record Office and are thus available for inspection by members of the general public.

Each of the courts will now be looked at in more detail.

> ✎ **EXAM TIP**
>
> Many students think that inferior courts are as unimportant as their name suggests. However, it is important to remember that the vast majority of cases are dealt with by the inferior courts. Most day-to-day court proceedings take place in the inferior courts and only a tiny proportion of these end up in the superior courts. This is a point that is worth making within any general essay that deals with the institutions of the legal system.

■ The jurisdictions of the courts and their personnel

> 📖 **REVISION NOTE**
>
> It will be useful to revise civil and criminal procedure in Chapters 6 and 7 alongside the jurisdictions of the courts as the two areas are inextricably linked. This chapter concentrates on the structure and jurisdictions of the courts and the personnel within them, whereas the chapter on civil and criminal procedure describes how a particular case can move from one court to another. As such there may be terms in this chapter that are better understood in terms of the criminal and civil procedures, so if you get confused by a particular term have a look in the section on procedure as it is likely to be explained in context there.
>
> It will also be useful to think about the personnel in each of these institutions as you work through their jurisdictions. This is dealt with in Chapter 5.

Magistrates' court

Criminal jurisdiction at first instance	All criminal proceedings begin in the magistrates' courts and well over 90% end there. The main types of hearing are: ■ Trial of summary offences and either-way offences ■ Bail applications ■ Issue of summonses and warrants for arrest or search ■ Youth Courts (formerly known as Juvenile Courts) for defendants between the ages of 10 and 18 ■ Mode of trial hearings ■ Committal proceedings for Crown Court trial or sentence

▶

Civil jurisdiction at first instance	Magistrates' courts have a limited civil jurisdiction, much of which concerns local government matters. The main categories of civil hearing include: ■ Highways, public health and licensing ■ Recovery of civil debts, such as National Insurance contributions and income tax ■ Family Proceedings Court – covers certain family or matrimonial matters (but not divorce) ■ Youth Court – care proceedings in respect of children
Personnel	■ Justices of the Peace (lay magistrates) – usually as a bench of three, or ■ A single district judge (magistrates' courts); these work on a full-time salaried basis and were formerly known as stipendiary magistrates ■ Assisted by clerk to the justices

✎ EXAM TIP

Students often forget that magistrates' courts have a civil jurisdiction. The popular image of magistrates' courts as only dealing with criminal cases is incorrect. If you have to discuss the function of a magistrates' court, remember to discuss the important role it has to play in civil matters too.

County court

Criminal jurisdiction at first instance	None
Civil jurisdiction at first instance	The jurisdiction to hear certain types of case may be limited geographically. The general types of case that may be heard in the county court include: ■ Contractual disputes (up to £5,000 in value) ■ Actions in tort (e.g. negligence and nuisance) where compensation sought for personal injuries is not more than £1,000 ■ Probate (administration of wills) ■ Divorce ■ Bankruptcy ■ Recovery of land ■ Some family proceedings ■ Equity matters (e.g. mortgages)

| Personnel | ■ Circuit judges |
| | ■ District judges |

Crown Court

Criminal jurisdiction at first instance	Technically, the prior intervention of the magistrates in committing defendants to the Crown Court for trial or sentencing means that neither of these jurisdictions are at first instance. However, it is probably easiest to consider the Crown Court to be a stage in the first-instance procedure. The Crown Court therefore deals with: ■ Trials on indictment (by jury) ■ Cases where the magistrates have declined jurisdiction before trial ■ Offences triable either way where the defendant has elected for trial by jury in the Crown Court ■ Referrals for sentence from the magistrates' court where the magistrates consider that their sentencing powers are inadequate for the case in question (there is a statutory limit on sentences in magistrates' courts of six months' imprisonment and/or £5,000 fine)
Appellate criminal jurisdiction	The Crown Court hears appeals from defendants against conviction or sentence or both in the magistrates' court
Civil jurisdiction at first instance	Limited so much as to be practically insignificant (e.g. certain disputes as to whether certain highways are in disrepair!)
Personnel	■ High Court judges (mainly QBD) ■ Circuit judges ■ Recorder (part-time) ■ Jury (for trials)

High Court

The High Court is one court. However, it is divided into three 'divisions' for administrative purposes. These are the

■ Queen's Bench Division;
■ Chancery Division; and
■ Family Division.

✎ **EXAM TIP**

Students often think that the three divisions of the High Court are different High Courts in some way. It is wrong (but very common) to say that 'there are three High Courts dealing with different matters'. There is just *one* High Court that is divided into three administrative areas.

Two or more judges sitting together may constitute a Divisional Court of the appropriate division. The Divisional Courts are not separate from the other courts. The entity often referred to as 'the Divisional Court' is more accurately referred to as the 'Divisional Court *of the Queen's Bench (or Chancery or Family) Division of the High Court'*.

Criminal jurisdiction at first instance	None of the Divisions has any practically significant criminal jurisdiction at first instance
Appellate criminal jurisdiction	*Queen's Bench Division* Criminal appeals from magistrates' courts by way of case stated and from Crown Court sitting without a jury (for example, a Crown Court hearing an appeal from the magistrates' court) *Chancery and Family Divisions* None
Civil jurisdiction at first instance	*Queen's Bench Division* ■ Contractual disputes (no upper limit on value) ■ Actions in tort (no upper limit on value) *Specialist subdivisions* ■ Administrative Court (applications for judicial review) ■ Admiralty Court (shipping and aircraft) ■ Commercial Court (banking, insurance and finance) ■ Election Court (disputed elections) ■ Technology and Construction Court (building construction related matters) *Chancery Division* ■ Disputes over wills, administration of estates and probate ■ Land actions ■ Mortgage actions ■ Trusts

- Company law
- Partnership actions
- Intellectual property (patents, trademarks and copyright)
- Bankruptcy
- Appointment of guardians

Specialist subdivisions

- Patents Court
- Court of Protection (disabled persons)

Family Division

- Defended divorce
- Adoption and wardship of children
- Some wills and probate cases

Appellate civil jurisdiction

Queen's Bench Division

- Appeals by way of case stated (as in criminal matters)

Chancery Division

- Various appeals from county courts (e.g. bankruptcy)

Family Division

- Appeals from the magistrates' court (in family cases)
- Appeals from Crown Court by way of case stated (in family cases)

Supervisory jurisdiction

Applications for judicial review in civil cases are generally heard by a single judge of the Queen's Bench Division. Approved applications for judicial review in criminal cases are usually heard by two (or occasionally three) judges of the Queen's Bench Division sitting as a Divisional Court

Personnel

- High Court judges (also known as *puisne* **judges** – pronounced 'puny' and meaning 'junior'; referred to in writing as, for example, Evans J)

Queen's Bench Division

- Head: Lord Chief Justice (referred to in writing as, for example, Smith LCJ)

Chancery Division

- (Effective) head: Vice-Chancellor (referred to in writing as, for example, Brown VC)

Family Division

- Head: President (referred to in writing as, for example, Jones P)

Knowing the names of the key personnel in the High Court (the Lord Chief Justice, Vice-Chancellor, and President of the Family Division) is a handy way to demonstrate that you take sufficient interest in the subject to know the actual individuals in the process and not just a selection of abstract roles. You might think that this is unimportant, but the law is administered by people – knowing who the key players are shows your examiner that you take a practical interest in the subject, which is always impressive.

Court of Appeal

Like the High Court, the Court of Appeal is also one court. It is divided into two divisions: the Civil Division and the Criminal Division. The Court of Appeal does not hear witnesses but instead considers legal argument and documentary evidence. The majority decision will prevail, so, in practice, an odd number of judges – usually three – sit. In certain cases of major public importance, sometimes five or even seven Lord Justices of Appeal will sit. Note that, although unlikely in practice, the court is properly constituted if only one judge sits.

Court of Appeal (Criminal Division)

Jurisdiction	The Court of Appeal (Criminal Division), as its name suggests, has an entirely appellate jurisdiction. The main cases dealt with are:
	■ Appeals from Crown Court by the defendant against conviction, sentence or a finding of fact
	■ References made by the Attorney-General following an **acquittal on indictment** under s. 36 of the Criminal Justice Act 1972 on a point of law (this is not an appeal by the prosecution as the Court of Appeal's findings will have no effect upon the defendant who will remain acquitted whatever happens). See Chapter 6 on Criminal Procedure
	■ References made by the Attorney-General under s. 36 of the Criminal Justice Act 1988 against an unduly lenient sentence
	■ Cases referred by the Criminal Cases Review Commission under s. 9 of the Criminal Appeal Act 1995 where there has been a possible miscarriage of justice
	■ Applications for leave to appeal to the Supreme Court
Personnel	■ Head: Lord Chief Justice (referred to in writing as, for example, Smith LCJ)
	■ 'Ordinary' judges: Lord or Lady Justices of Appeal (referred to in writing as, for example, Higgins LJ)
	■ Usually three judges (although the Civil Division is properly constituted with only one judge); sometimes five or seven (for particularly noteworthy cases); two judges may sit for an appeal by the defendant against sentence

Court of Appeal (Civil Division)

Jurisdiction	The Court of Appeal (Civil Division) deals with appeals from: ■ High Court ■ county courts ■ certain tribunals
Personnel	■ Head: The Master of the Rolls (referred to in writing as, for example, Stevens MR) ■ 'Ordinary' judges: Lord or Lady Justices of Appeal (referred to in writing as, for example, Peters LJ)

Supreme Court

The Supreme Court took over the judicial function of the House of Lords and became the highest court in the UK in October 2009. At the current time, for practical purposes, it is safe to assume that the Supreme Court has simply replaced the House of Lords and that whatever applied to the House of Lords applies equally well to the Supreme Court.

The Supreme Court of the United Kingdom was created by the Constitutional Reform Act 2005 and consists of twelve judges with a President and a Deputy President. The judges (other than the President and Deputy President) are styled 'Justices of the Supreme Court'. The Lords of Appeal in Ordinary became Justices of the Supreme Court; the senior Lord of Appeal in Ordinary became the President of the Court, and the second senior Lord of Appeal in Ordinary became the Deputy President of the Court.

It is located in Middlesex Guildhall on Parliament Square opposite the Houses of Parliament.

The Supreme Court does not hear evidence from witnesses but instead considers legal argument and documentary evidence.

Appellate criminal jurisdiction	The Supreme Court hears appeals in criminal cases from: ■ Court of Appeal (Criminal Division) ■ High Court (typically Queen's Bench Divisional Court) ■ Northern Ireland (not Scotland)
Appellate civil jurisdiction	The Supreme Court hears appeals in civil cases from: ■ Court of Appeal (Civil Division) ■ High Court (via the *leapfrog* procedure) ■ Scotland *and* Northern Ireland

▶

Other jurisdiction	To hear and determine questions relating to devolution (that is the competence of the executive and legislature in Scotland and Northern Ireland and of the Welsh National Assembly).
Personnel	Usually five or seven (but occasionally up to nine) Justices of the Supreme Court

The Judicial Committee of the Privy Council

The Privy Council is not, strictly speaking, a court at all. Since its function is to advise the Crown it cannot really be said to be 'deciding' cases. It may seem strange that what looks like an advisory body has any place in the English legal system at all. However, in practice, the 'advice' given to the Queen in the 'opinion' of the Judicial Committee of the Privy Council is almost always followed. As you will see from the table below, this may well be because of the seniority of its members.

When you revise the doctrine of judicial precedent in Chapter 4, you will see that decisions of the Judicial Committee of the Privy Council (usually referred to in this context simply as the 'Privy Council') are not binding on any domestic court, but are highly persuasive. Again, this is a result of the high judicial standing of its members.

Jurisdiction	The Judicial Committee of the Privy Council hears: ■ Appeals from certain Commonwealth countries ■ Appeals relating to disciplinary proceedings brought by various professions ■ Ecclesiastical appeals against pastoral schemes ■ Appeals against disciplinary decisions of the Royal College of Veterinary Surgeons
Personnel	At least three, and usually five, of the following: ■ Supreme Court Justices ■ Former Lords of Appeal in Ordinary ■ Lord President of the (Privy) Council and any former Lord Presidents ■ Members of the Privy Council with experience of high judicial office ■ Members of the Privy Council who are also Commonwealth judges

■ Courts of special jurisdiction

At the start of this chapter, some courts of special jurisdiction were mentioned. These were Coroners' Courts, and Courts Martial. To complete your revision of the institutions it is important that you consider these as well.

Some essay questions on the institutions may require you to discuss the role and operations of courts of special jurisdiction and consider their advantages and disadvantages. Just because you might not think of them as 'mainstream' does not mean that they will never appear in an exam question.

Coroners' Court

Jurisdiction	Coroners' Courts:
	■ Investigate the circumstances and causes of death

Courts Martial

Jurisdiction	Courts Martial:
	■ Deal with offences allegedly committed by members of the armed forces (think of them as military courts)

■ Putting it all together

Answer guidelines

See the sample question at the start of the chapter. A diagram illustrating how to structure your answer is available on the companion website.

Approaching the question

Although this question looks like a relatively straightforward descriptive essay covering civil and criminal appeals and the hierarchy of the courts, it does require some quite careful thought as to structure. One possible way to approach it might be to start at the Supreme Court and work down the hierarchy (as you might do for an essay on judicial precedent). However, since the question is focused on the appeals process, it would make more sense to start at the bottom and work up the hierarchy. You should also clearly separate civil and criminal routes of appeal. Again, this would make an easier structure for the examiner to follow.

▶

Important points to include

The following is one way in which you might approach the first part of the question:

- Identify that you need to cover civil and criminal courts separately.
- Start with civil courts and work up the hierarchy from county court to Supreme Court and explain the civil jurisdiction of each court in the hierarchy.
- Do the same for the criminal courts from the magistrates' court to the Supreme Court.
- This will then set you up for a structured discussion of the appeals process, to which you will return in Chapters 6 and 7.

 Make your answer stand out

- Give a clear introduction which explains to the examiner the approach and structure you are going to take and why you are going to consider civil and criminal courts separately.
- Don't forget that the magistrates' court has a civil jurisdiction as well.
- Be very clear when describing the operation of the High Court. The distinction between the Divisions of the High Court and the Divisional Courts of those Divisions can be tricky to articulate well, and very few students do so with clarity.

READ TO IMPRESS

Finch, E. and S. Fafinski (2011) *Legal Skills*, 3rd edn, Oxford: OUP.

Ingman, T. (2010) *The English Legal Process*, 13th edn, Oxford: OUP.

www.pearsoned.co.uk/lawexpress

 Go online to access more revision support including quizzes to test your knowledge, sample questions with answer guidelines, podcasts you can download, and more!

The doctrine of judicial precedent

4

Revision checklist

Essential points you should know:

☐ How to identify the material facts from a case or set of facts

☐ How to find the *ratio* of a case and distinguish this from the *obiter dicta*

☐ The hierarchy of the courts and how cases in each court are applied in the other courts in the hierarchy

☐ The content and effect of the 1966 Practice Statement

☐ How courts can avoid being bound by a difficult precedent

■ Topic map

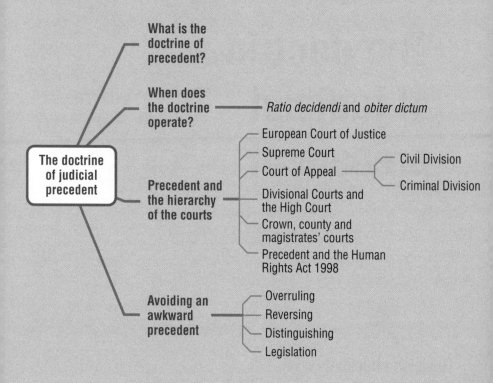

◼ Introduction

Decisions of higher courts carry more legal weight than decisions of lower courts

In the preceding chapter, you will have seen that the courts in the English legal system are organised in a hierarchy. Just as the courts at the top of the hierarchy are more 'important' than lower courts, the decisions of these courts carry more weight or have a higher legal 'value' than the decisions of lower courts. It is the doctrine of precedent, or *stare decisis*, that explains the way in which these decisions relate to each other.

For example, a case which is decided in the Court of Appeal could be relevant in three different directions: vertically up or down the hierarchy (Supreme Court and High Court respectively) and horizontally (other Court of Appeal cases). It is the doctrine of precedent that tells us in which types of case in which of the courts such a Court of Appeal decision would be relevant and how it would influence the outcome of the case being heard.

ASSESSMENT ADVICE

There are relatively limited ways in which an essay question on precedent could arise. They could typically focus on one of three areas:

- ◼ the operation of the doctrine of precedent itself;
- ◼ the ways in which judges might avoid following precedent and reasons why they may wish to do so;
- ◼ the advantages and disadvantages of the doctrine of precedent.

Understanding of the operation of precedent can often be tested by a problem question which presents a series of cases (real or fictitious) with questions as to whether or not the courts would be bound in particular factual situations. In this type of question it is vital to be clear which court a particular judgment came from, and to be methodical in working out whether or not it will bind another court. It is often not clear, so it is always important to remember to argue both sides before coming to a reasoned conclusion. Problem questions may often include matters of statutory interpretation mixed in with precedent (see Chapter 1).

Sample question

Could you answer this question? Below is a typical essay question that could arise on this topic. Guidelines on answering the question are included at the end of the chapter, whilst a sample problem question and guidance on tackling it can be found on the companion website.

ESSAY QUESTION

Outline the situations in which judges might avoid following a decision in an earlier case and discuss reasons why they may wish to do so.

What is the doctrine of precedent?

Stare decisis is a Latin phrase meaning 'let the decision stand' which means that once a decision has been reached in a particular case, it stands as good law and should be relied upon in other cases as an accurate statement of law. This is the essence of the doctrine of precedent.

The doctrine of precedent is based on the principle that *like cases should be treated alike*. This preserves *certainty* and *consistency* in the application of the law. This is important to our ideas of justice and fairness. We would think it questionable if judicial decisions were contradictory or if there was no logic to the pattern of their application.

Adherence to the doctrine of precedent also ensures that the law is sufficiently *flexible* to deal with novel situations and to ensure *justice* in each particular case. The operation of precedent means that the law can develop in line with the changes in society and that judicial decisions are in line with the morals and expectations of the community.

When does the doctrine operate?

The doctrine of precedent is based upon a series of presumptions:

- cases with the same or similar **material facts** (facts which are legally relevant) should be decided in the same way;

- decisions made in the higher level courts carry greater weight than those lower in the hierarchy. Therefore, a court is normally bound by courts which are higher or equal to them; and

- the legal reasons for the decision in the previous case (the *ratio decidendi*) must be identified and followed. These are distinct from any comments made in passing which are peripheral to the outcome of the case (*obiter dicta*).

A *binding precedent* is one that (generally) must be applied in a later case. It exists when the facts of a case are analogous with those of an earlier decision in a higher or equivalent court in which the applicable statement of law was part of the *ratio* of the earlier decision.

A *persuasive precedent* is one which is not binding (because it does not meet the criteria for a binding precedent set out above) but which contains other factors that mean that the decision is influential. A persuasive precedent can be followed (provided no binding precedent exists) but there is no compulsion on the courts to do so.

Binding precedent	Persuasive precedent
The facts in the decided case and the case before the courts must be sufficiently analogous to justify the imposition of the same legal principle/rule	The facts in the decided case and the case under consideration may have similar, but not directly analogous, facts
AND	OR
The decided case must have been heard in a court which is more senior in the hierarchy or at the same level as the court making the instant decision	The facts are analogous but the relevant legal rule is part of the *ratio* of a court that is lower in the hierarchy than the court making the decision
AND	OR
The part of the previous decision must be the *ratio* of the case rather than *obiter dicta*	The facts are analogous but the legal rule was part of the *obiter dicta* of a case heard in a higher or equivalent court
	OR
	The facts are analogous but the legal rule is part of the dissenting judgment of a case heard in a higher or equivalent court
	OR
	The facts are analogous but the legal rule is part of a judgment of a court outside of England and Wales. This includes decisions of the Privy Council (see Chapter 3)

Ratio decidendi and *obiter dicta*

The judgment in a case generally contains a statement of the facts and the relevant law and an explanation by the judge of the way in which the law applies to the particular situation before him and his conclusion as to the outcome of the case. The *ratio* of the case is the legal rule and associated reasoning that is essential to the resolution of the case. It is the conclusion that is reached by the application of the relevant legal rule to the material facts.

Therefore, in order to identify the *ratio* of a case, you must first isolate the material, or legally relevant, facts. Most judgments contain a wide general statement of the facts to establish the context in which the events occurred that gave rise to the case before the court. Many of these facts are not legally relevant – the outcome in the case would be the same even if these facts were different as they were not material to the legal question at the heart of the case. The ability to isolate the material facts from the legally irrelevant ones is an important skill to practise. See if you can identify the material facts from this scenario.

! Don't be tempted to . . .

You must take care when identifying the material facts.

Example

After an unlucky day at the races, Tony Sponge missed his train home. He decided to have a drink in the pub near the station while waiting for the next train, which was not due for three hours. During this time, Tony was befriended by another customer who offered to lend him a bicycle so that he did not have to wait for the train. Befuddled with alcohol, Tony fell off the bicycle a couple of times but persevered and was soon cycling happily along the road, singing away loudly. He was stopped by a policeman and charged with an offence under s. 12 of the Licensing Act 1872 which makes it an offence to be drunk whilst riding a carriage on a public highway.

Material facts

The defendant was riding a bicycle on a road whilst intoxicated.

Comment

These are the only facts which are pertinent to a determination of whether Tony is liable for the offence under s. 12 of the Licensing Act as the offence appears to have three key elements: (1) riding a carriage, (2) on a public highway, (3) whilst drunk.

Any other facts concerning Tony's previous activities, the ownership of the bicycle and his skill in riding the bike are not relevant to the determination of liability. Since they do not have any influence on the outcome of the case they are not material facts.

Accordingly, the *ratio* of the case will be the judicial reasoning that is used to conclude that Tony's activities fall within this offence. Given that it is clear that he was drunk and on a public highway, the *ratio* of the case will concern whether a bicycle is within the meaning of 'carriage' for the purposes of s. 12. Any comments that the judge may make about, for example, his views about drunken race-goers, the fact that the offence needs to be updated to reflect modern modes of transport or what he would have decided if the facts had been somewhat different, are not pertinent to the decision in the case and therefore are *obiter dicta*.

✎ EXAM TIP

The ability to extrapolate the *ratio* of a case is an important skill for a law student and one that will be useful throughout your degree. Take time to practise by reading cases in a range of subjects and extracting the **question of law** and using that to identify the material facts. This should allow you to attempt to extrapolate the *ratio* of the case from the judgment. Remember, the *ratio* is the legal reasoning used to reach a decision on the law in relation to the particular material facts of the case.

When trying to find the *ratio* of a judgment it sometimes helps to eliminate what is *obiter* first! Some useful ways to identify *obiter* statements are:

■ the discussion, explanation or reasoning of the judge is wider than that which is necessary to reach a decision on the facts of the case;

■ the judge hypothesises about the decision that he would have reached if the facts had been different;

■ the judge explains what his decision would have been in this case if he had not been compelled to reach a different decision owing to binding precedent; or

■ it is something said by a dissenting judge.

Before moving on to look at how precedent operates within the hierarchy of the courts, try to identify the *ratio* and *obiter* from the following (fictitious) transcript of Tony's case.

! Don't be tempted to . . .

You must be careful when identifying *ratio decidendi* and *obiter dicta*.

Parva LJ

I see no difficulty in finding that a bicycle is a carriage. At the time that the statute was enacted, a carriage was a common form of road transport just as a bicycle is today. Why, I'm told that there are six million bicycles in daily use in this country. It would be absurd if I were to find that such a means of transport was not within the scope of this section; it would allow every drunken wastrel who frittered away his money at the races to cycle with impunity irrespective of his potential to cause harm to other road users. It matters not what form of transport he adopted; my conclusion would be the same if he were riding a llama.

Crease LJ

I agree with my brother judge Parva in his finding that a bicycle is a carriage but I cannot agree with his statement that the section would apply had Sponge been riding a llama. It seems an unusual conclusion that a four-legged animal could be construed as a carriage. I would therefore conclude that a llama is not a carriage.

Clint LJ *(dissenting)*

I find it difficult to follow the reasoning of my brother judges. Indeed, I am somewhat affronted! A carriage is a means of transport that carries others and requires some means of propulsion such as a horse or an engine. That is not true of a bicycle. A bicycle is propelled by the rider and the rider alone so it is analogous to a horse, not a carriage. It is not legs or wheels that are pertinent here, but the means of propulsion. For that reason, I would uphold the appeal against conviction.

Comment

The *ratio* of Parva LJ's judgment is that a bicycle is a carriage. It is *obiter* that he would consider a llama to be a carriage, since this is merely his speculation on what his judgment would have been if the facts of the case had been different (of course, if Sponge *had* been riding a llama, this would be *ratio* rather than *obiter*!).

In agreeing with Parva LJ, the *ratio* of Crease LJ's judgment is also that a bicycle is a carriage. His discussion of the application of the section of the statute to a person on a llama is also *obiter*, as it is his speculation as to the outcome had the facts been different (it is also a discussion of Parva LJ's point which was, in itself, *obiter*!).

Clint LJ's view that a bicycle is not a carriage is *obiter*, as it is made in a dissenting judgment.

Therefore, the *ratio* of this case is simply that a bicycle is a carriage.

■ Precedent and the hierarchy of the courts

To recap then, the doctrine of precedent is concerned with the way that decisions in earlier cases are applied in subsequent cases (see Figure 4.1). The first steps in determining whether a precedent is binding or persuasive are to isolate the legally relevant facts and use them to distinguish between the *ratio* of the judgment and the *obiter dicta* as outlined above. Just because a statement is the *ratio* of an earlier case does not mean it is automatically binding in subsequent cases, just as the fact that a statement is *obiter* does not mean that

Figure 4.1

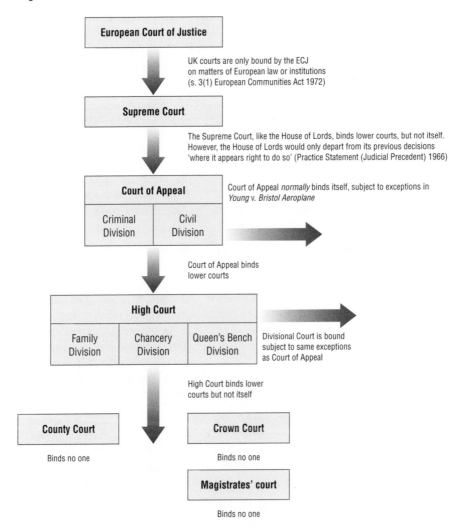

it has no precedent value – it all depends on the relationship between the court in which the original decision was made and the case in which the precedent is to be applied.

The general rule is that each court is bound by the decisions of those that are higher and of equivalent level in the hierarchy of the courts. For example, the Court of Appeal is normally bound by decisions of the Supreme Court (higher) and other Court of Appeal decisions (equivalent) (see Figure 4.1).

There are exceptions to this general rule regarding the hierarchy of the courts and the operation of precedent which will be addressed shortly. However, before considering these exceptions, make sure that you have a solid grasp of the basic rule by trying to predict how precedent would operate in the following example.

Imagine that the example given above involving a bicycle was to be applied in a later case. As the doctrine of precedent operates differently according to the level of the two courts involved, whether or not Parva LJ's *ratio* is binding precedent will depend upon the level of the court in which he made the original decision and the level of the court in which his statement is now being considered.

Original decision	Current case	Binding or persuasive?
Parva LJ's statement was made in the Supreme Court	The current case is being heard in the Court of Appeal and involves an appellant who was intoxicated whilst riding a bicycle on a public road	This is a straightforward example of a binding precedent. It involves the *ratio* of a decision made in a higher court being applied in a case with analogous facts.
Parva LJ's statement was made in the Supreme Court	The current case is being heard in the Supreme Court and involves an appellant who was intoxicated whilst riding a bicycle on a public road	Historically, this would have been a binding precedent as the House of Lords was bound by its own decisions. However, since 1966, the House of Lords has been able to depart from its own decisions. This principle currently also applies to the Supreme Court. This point will be discussed in further detail shortly.
Parva LJ's statement was made in the Court of Appeal	The current case is being heard in the Supreme Court and involves an appellant who was intoxicated whilst riding a bicycle on a public road	This is the application of the *ratio* of a case from a lower court being heard in a higher court so it is persuasive only. The Supreme Court may follow Parva LJ's statement but is not bound to do so.

Original decision	Current case	Binding or persuasive?
Parva LJ's statement was made in the Court of Appeal	The current case is being heard in the Court of Appeal and involves an appellant who was intoxicated whilst riding a llama on a public road	In this case, Parva LJ's statement would be *persuasive* authority as his statement about the llama was *obiter*. However, the Court of Appeal in the current case would also be considering that Crease LJ disagreed on this point, holding that a llama would not amount to a carriage (also *obiter*).
Parva LJ's statement was made in the Court of Appeal	The current case is being heard in the Divisional Court and involves an appellant who was intoxicated whilst riding a bicycle on a public road	This is a straightforward example of a *binding* precedent. It involves the *ratio* of a decision made in a higher court being applied in a case with analogous facts.

The European Court of Justice

The ECJ is not bound by its previous decisions, as it does not have the concept of *stare decisis*. However, it is strongly persuaded by its previous decisions. Following s. 3(1) European Communities Act 1972, UK courts are only bound by the ECJ on matters of European law or its institutions.

Supreme Court

For practical purposes, at present, it is safe to assume that whatever has been written about the operation of the doctrine of precedent in the House of Lords applies equally to the Supreme Court.

Until 1966 the House of Lords was bound by itself. This was known as the *London Tramways* rule (after *London Street Tramways Co Ltd* v. *London County Council* [1898] AC 375, HL) although the rule had been established before 1898.

The *London Tramways* rule was abolished by the *Practice Statement (Judicial Precedent)* [1966] 1 WLR 1234, HL made on behalf of the House of Lords by Lord Gardiner LC.

KEY STATEMENT

Practice Statement (Judicial Precedent) [1966] 1 WLR 1234, HL

Concerning: judicial precedent, House of Lords binding itself

Their Lordships regard the use of precedent as an indispensable foundation upon which to decide what is the law and its application to individual cases. It provides at least some degree of certainty on which individuals can rely in the conduct of their affairs, as well as a basis for orderly development of legal rules.

Their Lordships nevertheless recognise that too rigid adherence to precedent may lead to injustice in a particular case and unduly restrict the proper development of the law. They propose, therefore, to modify their present practice and while treating former decisions of this House as normally binding, to depart from a previous decision where it appears right to do so.

In this connection they will bear in mind the danger of disturbing retrospectively the basis upon which contracts, settlements of property and fiscal arrangements have been entered into and also the especial need for certainty in the criminal law. This announcement is not intended to affect the use of precedent elsewhere than in this House.

The Practice Statement 'does not mean that whenever . . . a previous decision was wrong, we should reverse it' (*Miliangos* v. *George Frank Textiles* [1976] AC 433, HL per Lord Cross). This shows that the House of Lords was extremely reluctant to use it, as it was acutely aware of the need for certainty and the dangers attached to departing from its previous decisions (as stated in the Practice Statement).

Therefore, it would only be used *where a previous decision caused injustices, caused uncertainty or hindered the development of the law*. Even if the Practice Statement might apply, the House of Lords still considered whether legislation might provide a better solution than departing from its previous decisions.

Examples

In *R* v. *Secretary of State for the Home Department, ex parte Khawaja* [1984] AC 74, HL it was held that, before departing from its own decisions, the House of Lords should be sure that:

- continued adherence to precedent involves the risk of injustice and would obstruct the proper development of the law; and

- departure from the precedent is the safe and appropriate way of remedying the injustice and remedying the law.

In *C (A Minor)* v. *Director of Public Prosecutions* [1996] AC 1, HL the House of Lords refused to abolish the presumption of *doli incapax* (the presumption that children under the age of 14 were incapable of criminal wrongdoing) despite finding it to be anomalous and absurd, preferring to call upon Parliament to remedy the situation.

Therefore, despite the freedom conferred by the Practice Statement to set aside its own decisions and exercise greater freedom in the development of the law, it is clear that the House of Lords was reluctant to exercise these powers. Nonetheless, as Lord Bridge stated in *R* v. *Shivpuri* [1987] 1 AC 1, HL in the first use of the Practice Statement in criminal law, 'the Practice Statement is an effective abandonment of our pretension to infallibility'.

✎ EXAM TIP

When tackling an essay or problem question involving the operation of precedent in the Supreme Court, it is important to make sure you demonstrate by mentioning some of the cases above that you understand that, despite the *Practice Statement*, the House of Lords did not usually follow it.

The Court of Appeal

Civil Division

The main principles concerning the circumstances in which the Court of Appeal (Civil Division) is bound by its previous decision were set out in *Young* v. *Bristol Aeroplane Co. Ltd* [1944] KB 718, CA.

KEY CASE

Young v. *Bristol Aeroplane Co. Ltd* **[1944] KB 718, CA**
Concerning: Court of Appeal bound by its own decisions

Legal principle
The Court of Appeal held that it is normally bound by its previous decisions, subject to three exceptions:

- **Where its own previous decisions conflict**. This may arise if the court in the later case was unaware of the decision of the earlier case: for instance, if the earlier case was very recent or unreported, or the second case might have distinguished the first, or one of the cases had been decided *per incuriam* (see below). In such situations, the Court of Appeal can choose which of its previous decisions to follow and which to reject. It may choose the earlier of the two decisions (*Starmark Enterprises Ltd*

▶

---

v. *CPL Distribution Ltd* [2002] Ch 306, CA). Whilst this has obvious implications for the future precedent value of the decision which is not followed, its status is not technically affected by the fact that it has not been followed; it could still be adopted in subsequent cases.

- **Where its previous decision had been implicitly overruled by the House of Lords**. This occurs when a previous Court of Appeal decision is inconsistent with a later House of Lords decision (e.g. *Family Housing Association* v. *Jones* [1990] 1 WLR 779, CA). This does not apply to the disapproval of the Privy Council (in *Re Spectrum Plus Ltd* [2005] 2 AC 680, HL). This could occur where a case has bypassed the Court of Appeal and gone straight to the House of Lords (by the 'leapfrog procedure' – see Chapters 6 and 7 on the appeals process).
- **Where its previous decision was made *per incuriam***. A decision made *per incuriam* is one made 'through carelessness' or without due regard to the relevant law. It should not be confused with *per curiam* which is a part of a judgment upon which all the judges are agreed.

Examples

There have been a number of cases which have considered what circumstances will render a decision *per incuriam*.

In *Morelle* v. *Wakeling* [1955] 2 QB 379, CA *per incuriam* decisions were defined as those 'given in ignorance or forgetfulness of some inconsistent statutory provision or of some authority binding on the court concerned . . .' – in other words, where the decision was reached without due regard for the correct law.

In *Duke* v. *Reliance Systems Ltd* [1988] QB 108, CA the court considered that 'if the court has failed to consider the relevant law, the decision will be *per incuriam* if the court *must* inevitably have reached a different decision had it considered the correct law; it will not suffice that the court *might* have reached a different decision had it considered the correct law'.

Criminal Division

All the exceptions from *Young* v. *Bristol Aeroplane* that apply in the Civil Division also apply to the Criminal Division. However, the Court of Appeal has a wider discretion in criminal cases where the liberty of the individual is at stake.

In *R* v. *Gould* [1968] 2 QB 65, CA, Lord Diplock stated:

if upon due consideration we were to be of the opinion that the law had been either misapplied or misunderstood in an earlier decision . . . we should be entitled to depart from the view as to the law expressed in the earlier decision notwithstanding that the case could not be brought within any of the exceptions laid down in *Young* v. *Bristol Aeroplane Co. Ltd.*

When applying precedents from the Court of Appeal in questions involving a criminal offence, remember to state that the Court has greater discretion to depart from previous decisions since the liberty of the individual is at stake.

There has been no ruling on whether the Civil and Criminal Divisions are bound by each other. However, their predecessors (the Court of Appeal and the Court of Criminal Appeal) were not. It is also accepted that, when dealing with criminal appeals, a 'full' Court of Appeal (five judges) can depart from decisions made by three judges.

The Divisional Courts and the High Court

The Divisional Courts (i.e. the Divisional Court of the appropriate division of the High Court for the particular matter) are bound by their own decisions subject to the same exceptions as the Civil Division of the Court of Appeal (i.e. primarily those in *Young* v. *Bristol Aeroplane*), and, arguably, the Criminal Division (following the decision in *R* v. *Greater Manchester Coroner, ex parte Tal* [1985] QB 67, DC). Decisions of the Divisional Courts are binding on the High Court. High Court decisions are not binding on the Divisional Courts (since the Divisional Courts operate at a higher level than the High Court by virtue of the nature of their jurisdiction, which is mostly to hear appeals).

Decisions of individual High Court judges are binding on lower courts but not on other High Court judges.

The Crown, county and magistrates' courts

The Crown Court is not bound by its previous decisions but, in order to promote certainty in the criminal law, is strongly persuaded by them. County and magistrates' courts are not bound by their own decisions and bind no other courts.

Precedent and the Human Rights Act 1998

Section 2 of the Human Rights Act 1998 requires future courts to take into account any previous decision of the European Court of Human Rights. Although these decisions are not formally binding, they are highly persuasive, which has major implications for the operation of the doctrine of precedent. The provision effectively allows the overruling of any previous English case authority that was in conflict with a previous decision of the European Court of Human Rights (for example, see *R (on the application of H)* v. *Mental Health Review Tribunal for North and East London* [2002] QB 1, CA, where the courts considered that part of the Mental Health Act 1983 was incompatible with Convention rights).

■ Avoiding an awkward precedent

The *Practice Statement* 1966 and the rule in *Young* v. *Bristol Aeroplane* give the House of Lords and Court of Appeal respectively the ability to avoid previous decisions of courts at the same level. In the case of the Court of Appeal, the circumstances in which the previous decisions of the Court of Appeal can be avoided are narrowly defined whereas the House of Lords exercises its power with caution because of the wider implications of departing from its own decisions in terms of the legal principle that results.

Other than by the operation of these particular rules, there are several methods that a court (at any level) can use to avoid an otherwise binding precedent. The approach taken depends upon whether the court which is confronted with the precedent wishes to merely avoid the precedent but to allow it to continue to exist as legal authority or whether the court wishes to deprive the precedent of any future legal effect.

Overruling

Overruling occurs when a court higher in the hierarchy overturns the decision of a lower court *in a different case*. This not only means that the higher court is not bound to follow the earlier decision but that it is negated of any legal force; indeed, it is regarded as never having been the law.

Reversing

Here, a court higher in the hierarchy overturns the decision of a lower court *in the same case*. For example, the House of Lords in *R* v. *Woollin* [1999] 1 AC 82, HL refused to follow the approach taken by the Court of Appeal in the same case, upholding the defendant's appeal against his conviction for murder and reversing the decision of the Court of Appeal definition of oblique intention.

Distinguishing

An alternative way in which an existing precedent that would otherwise be binding can be avoided is if the court decides that the case before them is *materially different*, either on the facts or on the point of law. By distinguishing in this way, the court is saying that they will not be applying the earlier case because it is not sufficiently similar to the case before them; the cases can be distinguished (on the facts or the law).

Legislation

Sometimes a precedent set by the courts is so problematic or controversial that Parliament will intervene to reverse it by emergency legislation. A recent example of this can be found in the High Court's decision in *R (on the application of Chief Constable of Greater Manchester*

Police) v. *Salford Magistrates' Court and Hookway* [2011] EWHC 1578 (Admin) in which the High Court upheld the ruling of the magistrates' court that the detention clock did not stop running when a suspect was bailed. This was contrary to that which had always been understood by police forces to be the case and had great ramifications for police procedure. The original judgment of the High Court was made on 19 May 2011: on 12 July 2011 the Police (Detention and Bail) Act 2011 received Royal Assent and effectively reversed the decision of the High Court. It gave clear statutory authority for the practices adopted by police forces prior to the High Court's decision. It also purports to be retrospective which is very unusual for legislation.

✎ EXAM TIP

In a problem question, always consider whether it is possible to avoid a precedent by distinguishing on the law or the facts. The question may ask you to give advice to someone who has been charged with a criminal offence where the precedents seem stacked against them. You will impress the examiner (and your client!) if you can think of ways in which earlier precedents can be avoided. An alternative to this approach is to interpret the *ratio* of the earlier case widely rather than narrowly so that there is greater scope to apply the authority but reach a decision which is consistent with what the judges want to achieve in the case. In many ways, it is true to say that the *ratio* of a case remains unclear until it is identified and applied by a later court.

■ Putting it all together

Answer guidelines

See the essay question at the start of the chapter. A diagram illustrating how to structure your answer is available on the companion website.

Approaching the question

There is more to this question than initially meets the eye. On the face of it, it simply involves a discussion of the ways in which an earlier precedent might be avoided which might lead you to discuss only the ideas of distinguishing, overruling and reversing. It is also important to remember that judges will also avoid following a decision from an earlier case if it is not binding upon them.

▶

Important points to include

- Discuss the operation of precedent in relation to the hierarchy of the courts.
- Make sure that you cover all possible courts.
- Identify the exceptions for each court, especially the House of Lords (*Practice Statement*) and the Court of Appeal (*Young* v. *Bristol Aeroplane*).
- Consider reasons why the courts may wish to avoid being bound. Key points to include here are:

  □ flexibility – the courts can develop the law without waiting for Parliament to legislate in response to changing views of society;
  □ justice and fairness – very old precedents may be outdated and have no place in today's society, yet a strict operation of the rules of precedent may lead to strange decisions;
  □ liberty – especially the flexibility that the Court of Appeal has in criminal cases.

 Make your answer stand out

- Give a clear introduction which explains to the examiner the approach and structure you are going to take.
- Explain the *Practice Statement* and *Young* v. *Bristol Aeroplane* in detail. Although there are only two absolutely essential authorities in this area, it is amazing how many students fail to explain them in sufficient depth (or at all!).
- Provide a thoughtful analysis of why judges may wish to choose to avoid being bound: this will demonstrate understanding as well as simple knowledge.
- Summarise the main points you have made in a focused conclusion.

READ TO IMPRESS

Cross, R. (1991) *Cross, Harris and Hart, Precedent in English Law*, 4th edn, Oxford: Clarendon.

Simpson, A. (1957 and 1958) 'The *ratio decidendi* of a case', 20 *Modern Law Review* 413; 21 *Modern Law Review* 155.

Wright, L. (1943) 'Precedent', 8 *Cambridge Law Journal* 118.

www.pearsoned.co.uk/lawexpress
Go online to access more revision support including quizzes to test your knowledge, sample questions with answer guidelines, podcasts you can download, and more!

Personnel

Revision checklist

Essential points you should know:

- [ ] The roles of each of the various personnel within the legal system
- [ ] The constitutional reason for judicial independence and the means in which it is protected
- [ ] The process by which juries are drawn from the general public and the challenges that might be made by the prosecution or defence against potential jurors
- [ ] Criticisms of the legal profession, the judiciary, magistrates and the jury and the effects of any potential reforms

■ Topic map

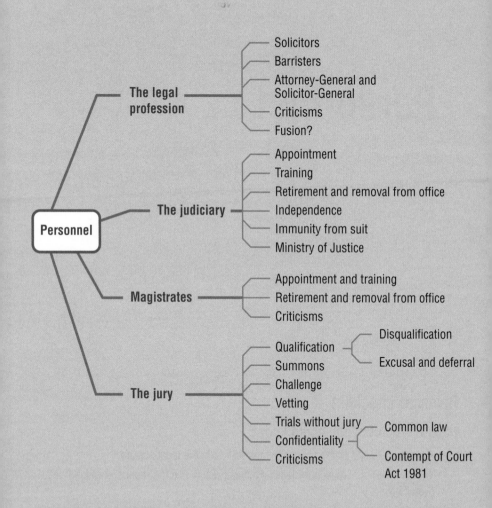

■ Introduction

The legal system has people performing many different roles

This chapter is concerned with the people involved within the English legal system. These include solicitors and barristers, magistrates and judges and the jury. Although knowledge of the roles of each of these individuals is fundamentally important to your overall understanding of the legal system, we will also consider the advantages and disadvantages of the way in which some of these roles operate. Therefore, when revising this area it is important to ask yourself questions about the personnel in the social and legal context in which they operate.

ASSESSMENT ADVICE

The personnel of the legal system provides tremendous scope for examiners. There is always debate around each area covered in this chapter which can be reflected in the form of a 'broad issue' essay question. You should use this chapter as a means of consolidating the material you have covered on your course and revisit any further reading on potential reforms and pros and cons of each area in a range of sources. Look for any particularly recent developments. Remember that it is the skill to demonstrate awareness and ability in terms of critical and analytical thought that will set you apart in an examination.

The scope for setting problem questions on the personnel within the English legal system is quite limited, even for the most inventive examiner. However, you might wish to look back at past examination papers to see if you can find a problem question on this topic, just in case.

■ Sample question

Could you answer this question? Below is a typical essay question that could arise on this topic. Guidelines on answering the question are included at the end of the chapter, whilst a sample problem question and guidance on tackling it can be found on the companion website.

ESSAY QUESTION

Trial by jury has no place in modern Britain.

Critically analyse this statement.

■ The legal profession

One of the most notable aspects of the English legal profession is that it is traditionally divided into two branches, so that lawyers are either *solicitors* or *barristers*. Each branch of the profession has its own structure and organisation, training requirements, procedures, customs and practices. The structure of the legal profession often comes under criticism and such criticisms could easily form the content of an essay question. It is important to understand the way in which each branch of the profession operates, in order to understand and critically analyse the comments on its structure and possible proposals for reform that may be raised in the exam.

Solicitors

Solicitors are generally the first port of call for individuals seeking legal advice. As such, solicitors may deal with a wide variety of legal issues, although it can be misleading to think of them as the 'general practitioners' of the legal profession. Many solicitors, particularly in larger firms, are specialists in particular fields. Solicitors are permitted to practise in partnerships: the vast majority do so, although some work in local authorities, governmental institutions, or 'in-house' in large companies. The majority of partnership practices are quite small: around five partners in a single office location. There are currently around 140,000 qualified solicitors of whom 110,000 are actually practising. Of those in practice, around 40% (44,000) are women.

Qualification and training

The steps to qualification as a solicitor are illustrated in Figure 5.1.

The first step in the route to qualification as a solicitor is either completing a qualifying law degree or a non-law (or non-*qualifying* law) degree followed by the one-year Common Professional Examination (CPE) – this is effectively an intensive course in the law for non-law graduates which covers the seven foundations of legal knowledge required for a qualifying law degree (EU law, constitutional and administrative law, criminal law, contract law, tort law, land law and equity and trusts). After this, there is a one-year Legal Practice Course (LPC) followed by a term (typically two years) as a trainee solicitor within a firm.

The Law Society

The Law Society is the representative body for solicitors in England and Wales. Its aims are to 'help, protect and promote solicitors across England and Wales'. It does this by negotiating with and lobbying the profession's regulators, Government and others and by offering training and advice.

Solicitors Regulation Authority

The Solicitors Regulation Authority (SRA) deals with all regulatory and disciplinary matters, and sets, monitors and enforces standards for solicitors across England and Wales. Formerly known as the Law Society Regulation Board, it acts solely in the public interest.

Figure 5.1

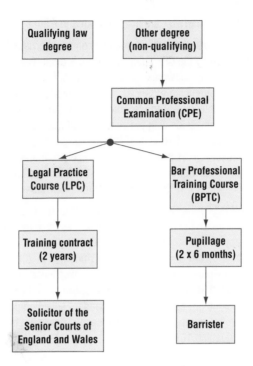

Legal Complaints Service

The Legal Complaints Service (LCS) is for members of the public wishing to make a complaint about solicitors. Formerly known as the Consumer Complaints Service, this independent and impartial body works with solicitors to resolve issues. It handles over 300 calls a day on a range of legal complaints.

Barristers

Barristers are typically thought of as advocates – those that speak in court. However, the role of the barrister also includes a great deal of time out of court, drafting arguments and pleadings and writing advices for solicitors. Unlike solicitors, barristers are not permitted to work in partnerships, except with lawyers from overseas. Instead, most barristers work in a set of chambers; that is, a set of shared offices serviced by a clerk who manages the work of the chambers. Barristers of three years' call may practise independently. Since 2004, barristers (again, of at least three years' call) have been allowed to take instructions directly from members of the public.

Qualification and training

The steps to qualification as a barrister are also illustrated in Figure 5.1.

As with solicitors, the first step in the route to qualification as a barrister is either a law degree or a non-law degree followed by the CPE. After this, there is a one-year Bar Professional Training Course (BPTC) (formerly known as the Bar Vocational Course or BVC, to which many people still refer). Before commencing the BPTC, students must join one of the four Inns of Court in London (Middle Temple, Inner Temple, Lincoln's Inn and Gray's Inn); during the BPTC they must also familiarise themselves with the customs and tradition of the Bar, and must dine at their Inn twelve times. The BPTC is then followed by a further one-year pupillage for barristers intending to practise: in essence an apprenticeship to a practising barrister. This is taken as two 'sixes': that is, six-month periods. The first of these will typically involve training with a barrister; the second may involve the pupil in some work, albeit limited.

Top barristers are appointed by the Crown to the rank of Queen's Counsel (QC), usually referred to as 'silks' by virtue of the (partially) silk gown they have earned the right to wear. A new process for the appointment of QCs was developed by the Bar Council and the Law Society and approved by the Lord Chancellor in 2004 (modified in 2006). It aims to ensure that there is a 'fair and transparent means of identifying excellence in advocacy in the higher courts'. The process is based around a competency framework that barristers are expected to demonstrate and decisions are made by an independent selection panel (rather than solely by the Lord Chancellor as was previously the case). There are currently around 1,000 barristers of QC status, of which 10% are women.

The Bar Council and the Bar Standards Board

The General Council of the Bar of England and Wales and of the Inns of Court (generally referred to as the Bar Council, for convenience) is the representative body for barristers. The conduct of barristers is independently regulated by the Bar Standards Board, which was established in 2006. Its aim is to promote and maintain excellence in the quality of legal services provided by barristers. The Code of Conduct of the Bar of England and Wales sets out the practising requirements, fundamental principles and standards of expected conduct for barristers.

One of the provisions of the Code is the 'cab rank rule', which means that a barrister must not decline to accept instructions in a case unless to do so would cause them professional embarrassment, for example, if it concerns an area of law outside of their competence, if they are unavailable due to other professional commitments, or if they have a connection with the case that would make it difficult for them to maintain their professional independence.

The Attorney-General and the Solicitor-General

The Attorney-General and his deputy, the Solicitor-General, are legal advisers to the Crown. They are usually barristers and members of the House of Commons (although sometimes the House of Lords); the Attorney-General is a member of Government.

The Attorney-General's role includes:

- advising Government departments on matters of law;
- representing the Crown in civil proceedings;
- representing the Crown in criminal proceedings involving constitutional or political allegations (e.g. treason);
- representing the public interest in criminal matters.

Criticisms

> ✎ **EXAM TIP**
>
> There are a number of common criticisms of the legal profession upon which you should have your own opinions. This section will list the most common in outline, but you should give each of them further thought as you go through, because simply repeating them may come across as somewhat unthinking and trite. Consider whether you agree or disagree with each one. Then think *why* that is. A discussion of criticisms of the legal profession could arise as part of a potential essay – it is, therefore, important to have your own opinion and to be able to articulate it clearly. It is, however, always useful to consider some academic comment which you may have encountered on your course.

Solicitors	Barristers
Under-representation of women?	Under-representation of women?
Under-representation of ethnic minorities?	Under-representation of ethnic minorities?
Unequal treatment of women/ethnic minorities in terms of career progression/pay?	Attainment of the rank of QC is an unfair means of charging higher fees?

Fusion?

Possible arguments for fusion	Possible arguments against fusion
Solicitors perform advocacy work, especially in lower courts and tribunals (there is a statutory right for solicitors to appear in magistrates' and county courts and, rarely, depending on location, in the Crown Court)	A fall in the quality of advocacy

▶

Possible arguments for fusion	Possible arguments against fusion
Barristers perform pleadings and write draftings	Smaller firms may go out of business
Two professionals are not needed where one could do just as well – Costs? Delay? Efficiency?	Reduced number of specialist advocates
	Judges need to have confidence in the quality of the advocates before them
	Independence of the Bar ensures fair defences available to all
	The Benson Royal Commission on Legal Services (1979) unanimously rejected the idea of fusion
It is arguable that some degree of fusion has been organised via the Courts and Legal Services Act 1990 and the Access to Justice Act 1999	

✎ EXAM TIP

Another controversial area arises from the notion of 'fusion' – whether the two branches of the profession should be combined into one. This could give rise to a discursive essay problem. Again, you should consider your own opinion and any *substantiated* arguments for and against.

The Courts and Legal Services Act 1990

Amongst other things, this Act abolished the monopolies that solicitors had over property conveyancing (by establishing Licensed Conveyancers), probate work and the rights to conduct litigation.

The Access to Justice Act 1999

The rights of audience of lawyers before the courts were overhauled by the Access to Justice Act 1999. This effectively abolished the Bar's monopoly to rights of audience in the higher courts. The key sections of this Act are as follows:

Section	Effect and comment
36	All barristers have rights of audience in all courts. All solicitors have rights of audience and rights to conduct litigation in all courts provided that solicitors obey the necessary rules of conduct and have completed the training requirements, or obtained a higher-courts advocacy qualification.
37	Prohibits restrictions on rights of audience for employed lawyers. The biggest practical implication of this is that the CPS may use employed advocates in the higher courts – criticised by the Bar which fears a possible lack of impartiality on the part of CPS lawyers.
39	Ensures portability of audience rights between professions.
42	Establishes the primacy of an advocate's ethical duties to the court and to act in the interest of justice over any other civil law obligations.

Standards of legal services

The courts traditionally held that barristers and solicitors could not be liable for claims in tort for negligent legal advice or advocacy (*Rondel* v. *Worsley* [1969] 1 AC 191, HL; *Saif Ali* v. *Sydney Mitchell & Co* [1980] AC 198, HL). However, this position was changed by the House of Lords in *Arthur JS Hall & Co.* v. *Simons* [2002] 1 AC 615, HL such that barristers (and solicitors) can be sued in negligence for poor advocacy or conduct of litigation. Lord Hoffmann commented (before dismissing the appeal) that:

> I have now considered all the arguments relied upon in *Rondel* v. *Worsley* [1969] 1 AC 191. In the conditions of today, they no longer carry the degree of conviction which would in my opinion be necessary to sustain the immunity. The empirical evidence to support the divided loyalty and cab rank arguments is lacking; the witness analogy is based upon mistaken reasoning and the collateral attack argument deals with a real problem in the wrong way. I do not say that *Rondel* v. *Worsley* [1969] 1 AC 191 was wrongly decided at the time. The world was different then. But, as Lord Reid said then, public policy is not immutable and your Lordships must consider the arguments afresh.

The judiciary

As well as revising the roles of solicitors and barristers who prepare and present cases, you also need to make sure that you understand the role of the judiciary within the legal system.

> **□ REVISION NOTE**
>
> When revising the judiciary, you may find it useful to go back to Chapter 3 and remind yourself of the court hierarchy – in particular, the distinction between *superior* and *inferior* courts, and the types of judge that may sit in each court.

Appointment

The procedure for judicial appointments was overhauled by the Constitutional Reform Act 2005, which addressed a number of important areas, including:

- *Judicial independence*: The Act imposes a duty on Government to uphold the independence of the judiciary.

- *Reforming the office of Lord Chancellor*: The Act reformed the post of Lord Chancellor, transferring his judicial functions to the President of the Courts of England and Wales. The Lord Chief Justice became President of the Courts of England and Wales. He is responsible for the training, guidance and deployment of judges. He will also represent the views of the judiciary of England and Wales to Parliament and ministers.

- *Judicial Appointments Commission*: The Act established an independent Commission, responsible for selecting candidates to recommend for judicial appointment to the Lord Chancellor. This ensures that while merit remains the sole criterion for appointment, the appointments system is placed on a fully modern, open and transparent basis (see www.judicialappointments.gov.uk).

> **□ REVISION NOTE**
>
> Given that the Constitutional Reform Act 2005 implemented significant reform, it will be worth looking in the news (and, of course, within your course materials) to see if anything noteworthy has transpired since its coming into force. Visit the website of the England and Wales judiciary at www.judiciary.gov.uk for further details. The website also contains some useful interactive learning resources which could be used for further revision.

Training

All judicial training is the responsibility of the Judicial Studies Board (JSB) (see www.jsboard.co.uk), established in 1979. It is directly responsible for the development and delivery of training to judges in the Crown, county and higher courts. It also provides some direct training to tribunals judges and those exercising judicial functions in the magistrates' courts, as well as training materials, advice and support to those who train magistrates.

Prior to that, judges received minimal or no training, unlike European judges, who undergo specialist and extensive training. In Europe, being a judge is an early career choice rather than a possible progression following a career in advocacy. Despite common criticisms that there is insufficient training of the judiciary, the introduction of the Human Rights Act 1998 and the Civil Procedure Rules 1998 led to a flurry of training activity.

The 1993 Runciman Commission Report also made recommendations relating to training, including:

- the need for more resources (primarily money) to be given to training;
- periodic 'refresher' training;
- a system of appraisals by other judges;
- the opportunity for members of the Bar to provide feedback on judges;
- increased awareness of race and gender issues.

Retirement and removal from office

Retirement	All judges are required to retire at 70, although they may continue in office at the discretion of the Lord Chancellor (s. 11, Senior Courts Act 1981).
Higher courts – security of tenure during good behaviour	Judges of the Supreme Court, Court of Appeal and the High Court hold office during 'good behaviour', subject to the proviso that they can be removed by the Crown on the presentation of an address by both Houses of Parliament (s. 11, Senior Courts Act 1981; s. 6, Appellate Jurisdiction Act 1876 relates to the House of Lords). This procedure has, however, never been used in relation to an English judge (although it was used in 1830 to remove an *Irish* judge, Sir Jonah Barrington, who had misappropriated £700 of court funds).
Circuit judges	Circuit judges below the High Court can be removed on grounds of incapacity or misbehaviour by the Lord Chancellor without the requirement to gain Parliamentary approval (s. 17, Courts Act 1971). However, despite this, the only judge so removed was Campbell J (1983) convicted for evading customs duty on cigarettes and whisky.
District judges	District judges (magistrates' courts) may be dismissed by the Lord Chancellor on grounds of incapacity or misbehaviour (s. 22, County Courts Act 1984).
Infirmity	High Court or Court of Appeal judges too infirm to resign themselves may be removed from office by the Lord Chancellor (s. 11, Senior Courts Act 1981).

Independence of the judiciary

Within the framework of our constitution, judges must be independent; they must deliver judgment with complete impartiality without bias, interference of personal preference or any pressure from political forces or the parties appearing before them. This notion is upheld by a number of legal and conventional means. It is particularly difficult to remove senior judges from office (see table above): they are also protected by the doctrine of *judicial immunity from suit*.

Immunity from suit

Judges of *superior courts* cannot be sued in respect of acts done in their judicial capacity in good faith. This applies even if a judge has acted mistakenly or in ignorance of his powers. This enables judges to perform their duties without fear of adverse consequences and is an important means of upholding judicial impartiality. This was extended to magistrates (both lay magistrates and district judges (magistrates' courts)) by the Courts and Legal Services Act 1990 and is currently provided by s. 31 of the Courts Act 2003.

Ministry of Justice

The Ministry of Justice (www.justice.gov.uk) was launched in May 2007 and is responsible for the courts, prisons, probation, criminal law and sentencing. It was created from the Department of Constitutional Affairs, Her Majesty's Courts Service, the Tribunals Service and the National Offender Management Service. The Lord Chancellor is also the Secretary of State for Justice.

 Make your answer stand out

There is a wide variety of issues concerning the judiciary, so you must think critically when revising the material in this section. There are several questions to consider as you go through, any of which could form a challenging essay in an exam:

- Should there be more specialist judges?
- Are judges sufficiently well trained?
- Should the methods of selecting, appointing and promoting members of the judiciary be reformed? If so, how?
- Is the social composition of the judiciary appropriate in modern Britain?
- Are judges competent to make law? Should they do so?
- Since judges are usually former barristers, do you think this gives rise to undue conscious or subconscious influence?

◼ Magistrates

Magistrates, also known as Justices of the Peace, carry out their duties locally and deal with most criminal cases. They consider the evidence in each case and reach a verdict. If a defendant is found guilty, or pleads guilty, they decide on the most appropriate sentence. Magistrates deal with the less serious criminal cases, such as minor theft, criminal damage, public disorder and motoring offences. Around 92% of all criminal cases in England and Wales are dealt with by magistrates.

KEY DEFINITION: Magistrates

The term magistrates encompasses *lay magistrates* and *district judges (magistrates' courts)*. Although it is often used to mean just lay magistrates, it is important to recognise that the term can cover district judges (magistrates' courts) as well. The title *justice of the peace* covers both lay magistrates and district judges (magistrates' courts).

	Lay magistrates	District judges (magistrates' courts)
How many?	Around 28,000 (virtually equal split between men and women)	Around 130
Legal qualification?	Not usually. Magistrates are assisted and advised by clerks (note that there is no current requirement for magistrates' clerks to be legally qualified)	Professionally legally qualified (with a seven-year 'general qualification' – s. 71, Courts and Legal Services Act 1990)
Time?	Part-time (but at least 26 half-day sittings per year; maximum 100 sittings per year)	Full-time
Payment?	Unpaid, but receive allowances for travel, subsistence and loss of earnings	Salaried
Bench?	Usually sit in twos or threes	Sit alone
Jurisdiction?		Identical
Location?	Outer London and the rest of the country	Primarily inner London

Appointment and training

Lay magistrates are appointed by the Lord Chancellor on behalf of the Queen. These appointments are made after consultation with local advisory committees; there is one of these committees in each county, each of which is usually chaired by the Lord Lieutenant for that county. Candidates may be nominated by local bodies, such as political parties, unions, chambers of commerce and federations of local business. The committee may also advertise for candidates. Candidates may then be interviewed, before the names of those deemed appropriate by the committee are given to the Lord Chancellor, who has the final say on appointments.

There is a statutory requirement upon the Lord Chancellor for the training, development and appraisal of lay magistrates (s. 19, Courts Act 2003), much of which is gained through practical experience in the courtroom. The training is also aimed at emphasising equal treatment of defendants irrespective of their race, sex, religion, disability or sexual orientation. It also covers basic law and procedure, the rules of evidence and the principles of sentencing. New magistrates are also given a mentor who provides formal and informal feedback on performance and identifies any further training needs.

Retirement and removal from office

'Retirement'	Lay magistrates do not 'retire'; they are entered on the 'supplemental list' at the age of 70 (or in the event of incapacity or by application) (s. 13, Courts Act 2003). Lay magistrates on the supplemental list are no longer qualified to act in the capacity of justice of the peace.
District judges (magistrates' courts)	District judges (magistrates' courts) may be dismissed by the Lord Chancellor on grounds of incapacity or misbehaviour (s. 22, Courts Act 2003). District judges (magistrates' courts) are required to vacate their office on reaching the age of 70 (s. 76, Judicial Pensions and Retirement Act 1993).
Lay magistrates	Lay magistrates may be dismissed by the Lord Chancellor on grounds of incapacity, misbehaviour, incompetence or neglect of duty (s. 11, Courts Act 2003). Prior to the Courts Act 2003, the Lord Chancellor did not have to show cause for removal.

Criticisms

There are a number of criticisms which can be aimed at the lay magistracy. These are predominantly aimed at its political and social composition leading to fears that, despite the requirement for independence, lay magistrates are 'only people' and might be swayed by their own personal judgment about the 'badness' of a case. Lay magistrates will have personal prejudices, and despite a campaign to recruit new lay magistrates to change the socio-economic composition of the bench, lay magistrates still primarily come from a narrow section of society; this may result from the frequency of work required (minimum thirteen days per year) and its largely unpaid nature.

 Make your answer stand out

As with the judiciary, there are a number of potential discussion areas surrounding the lay magistracy that could give rise to an essay question. When revising you may wish to refer back to your course materials for greater depth of information around questions such as:

■ What measures could be taken to change the socio-economic composition of the lay magistracy?
■ What are the advantages and disadvantages of replacing the lay magistracy with full-time salaried judges?

■ The jury

Juries are most often used in criminal proceedings in the Crown Court, although they may also be used in coroners' courts and (rarely) in civil proceedings (malicious prosecution, false imprisonment, fraud and defamation cases). This section will focus predominantly on their more familiar use in criminal trials.

Qualification

The eligibility criteria for jury service were amended by the Criminal Justice Act 2003, which abolished most former categories for ineligibility (most significantly members of the legal profession), leaving the qualification criteria under s. 1 of the Juries Act 1974 (as substituted) as:

■ aged between 18 and 70 and registered as an elector;

■ ordinarily resident in the UK, Channel Islands or Isle of Man for at least five years (since age 13);

■ *not* mentally disordered; and

■ *not* disqualified or excused from jury service.

Disqualification

Persons *disqualified* from jury service are as follows:

■ persons on bail;

■ persons who *at any time* have been sentenced to imprisonment for five years or more;

- persons who in the last ten years have:
  - ☐ served any sentence;
  - ☐ received a suspended sentence;
  - ☐ received a community rehabilitation order;
  - ☐ received a community punishment order;
  - ☐ received a drug treatment and testing or a drug abstinence order.

Excusal and deferral

The following are *excused* from jury service:

- persons who have served or attended to serve on a jury in the past two years;
- full-time serving members of the armed forces if certified by their Commanding Officer that their absence would prejudice the efficiency of the service;
- those who *at the discretion of the Jury Central Summoning Bureau (JCSB)* show 'good reason' – such as illness, pre-arranged holiday commitments, difficulties with childcare arrangements, work commitments, study commitments or personal involvement in the facts, or with a party or witness in the particular case;
- attendance may be *deferred* at the JCSB's discretion for similar 'good reason'.

Judges may also excuse a person whom they doubt will be able to act effectively as a juror because of his insufficient understanding of English, or any physical disability (such as deafness or blindness) (ss. 9B and 10, Juries Act 1974).

Summons

The JCSB operates a centralised system (based at Blackfriars Crown Court in London) which randomly selects potential jurors from the electoral register, issues summonses and deals with responses from jurors. This centralised system was established after a successful pilot scheme and attempts to address concerns relating to adequacy of representation and equality of treatment.

The court officer produces lists (known as 'panels') of jurors, from which particular juries are selected by ballot in open court and then sworn in individually.

Since the power to summon jurors is an administrative matter, it follows that judges may not order multiracial juries to be constructed artificially (*R* v. *Smith* [2003] 1 WLR 2229, CA) or bring in jurors outside the normal catchment area in an attempt to minimise juror intimidation (*R* v. *Ford* [1989] QB 868, CA; *R* v. *Tarrant* [1998] Crim LR 342, CA).

Challenge

A defendant may challenge any or all of the jurors *for cause* (i.e. good reason) after the juror's name (or number) has been balloted. Any challenges for cause will be tried by the trial judge in preliminary hearings.

The prosecution may also challenge for cause. Furthermore, it may 'stand by' any potential juror (and if necessary the whole panel) *without reasons*. In theory, 'standing by' represents a provisional challenge for which cause should subsequently be given; however, in practice, there are usually enough acceptable jurors in the pool from which to form a jury, and the cause for the provisional challenge is never investigated. There were fears that this imbalance of power was being misused by prosecutors; this led to the Attorney-General's *Practice Note (Juries: Right to Stand By: Jury Checks)* [1988] 3 All ER 1086, effectively mandating that the right be used sparingly and only in exceptional circumstances:

- where a juror is 'manifestly unsuitable' (and the defence agrees that exercise of the right is appropriate);
- where the Attorney-General has personally authorised use of the right of stand by following the outcome of a jury check in a trial concerning terrorism or national security (see Vetting below).

Vetting

The Attorney-General's 1988 Guidelines on Jury Checks provide certain exceptional circumstances in cases of national security (where the evidence will predominantly be heard **in camera** – that is 'in private') or terrorism where vetting of individual jurors may be personally authorised by the Attorney-General.

KEY DEFINITION: *In camera*

Proceedings *in camera* are held in *private*, without members of the public present. Don't confuse this with *on camera* – televised broadcasts of court proceedings are prohibited!

Vetting involves criminal record checks and the potential involvement of the security services. The outcome of a check may justify the exercise of the prosecution right to stand by if, according to the guidelines, there is a *strong* reason for believing that the juror may be:

- a risk to security;
- susceptible to improper approaches;
- unduly influenced.

Make your answer stand out

When revising the judiciary and lay magistracy, you should have referred back to your course materials for greater depth in some of the areas which could give rise to essay questions. The jury system also gives rise to a number of questions, any of which could appear as a potential essay, such as:

■ Does the way in which jurors are selected adequately represent the population as a whole?
■ Do you think the rights to challenge potential jurors are fair and balanced?
■ Do you think that jury vetting is a violation of an individual's right to privacy?

Trials without jury

The most prominent issue at present concerns the abolition of the right to a jury trial in certain cases. In 1986, the Roskill Report advocated the abolition of the right to jury trial in complex fraud cases, as did the Auld Committee in 2001. These proposals were adopted by the Government in s. 43 of the Criminal Justice Act 2003, which gave prosecutors the power to apply for serious and/or complex fraud trials to be conducted without a jury. Permission would be granted if:

> The complexity of the trial or the length of the trial (or both) is likely to make the trial so burdensome to the members of a jury hearing the trial that the interests of justice require that serious consideration should be given to the question of whether the trial should be conducted without a jury.

Due to the controversial nature of this provision, it could not be implemented without an affirmative resolution in the House of Commons and the House of Lords (s. 330(5)(b), Criminal Justice Act 2003). Despite the Government's commitment to the introduction of s. 43, there was lack of support for its introduction, especially in the House of Lords, so the Government sought to achieve the abolition of the right to jury trial in complex fraud cases by introducing specific legislation in the form of the Fraud (Trials without a Jury) Bill 2006. A detailed outline of the Government's arguments in favour of the Bill can be found in the *Fraud (Trial without a Jury) Bill Research Paper* (06/57). The Bill did not find support in the House of Lords and did not proceed.

However, a similar provision that curtails the right to jury trial in cases where there is a serious risk of jury tampering did not receive such opposition and came into force on 24 July 2007. Section 44 of the Criminal Justice Act 2003 allows the judge, following an application by the prosecution, to order that a trial should proceed at Crown Court without a jury if two conditions are satisfied:

■ There is evidence of real and present danger that jury tampering would take place: s. 44(4).

■ Notwithstanding any steps (including the provision of police protection) which might reasonably be taken to prevent jury tampering, the likelihood that it would take place would be so substantial as to make it necessary in the interests of justice for the trial to be conducted without a jury: s. 44(5).

Section 44(6) gives three examples of situations that might present a real and present danger of jury tampering:

- A retrial of a case in which the jury at the previous trial were discharged due to tampering.
- A case in which tampering has taken place in previous proceedings involving the defendant or any of the defendants.
- Cases in which there has been intimidation or attempted intimidation of any person likely to be a witness in the trial.

In cases where the judge makes an order that the case can proceed without a jury, this decision can be appealed to the Court of Appeal in an attempt to restore the defendant's right to trial by jury. On 18 June 2009, the court rejected such an application in *R* v. *T* [2009] EWCA Crim 1035 and ruled that the trial of the four defendants who were charged with an armed robbery at Heathrow Airport in February 2004 would be heard by a judge only. The trial commenced in January 2010.

Confidentiality

Common law

At common law, jury deliberations take place in private and must remain confidential after the trial. In other words, after the case is concluded the court will not admit evidence about, or enquire into, what transpired in the jury room. A series of cases which demonstrate the application of the common law principle are:

- *R* v. *Miah (Badrul)* [1997] 2 Cr App R 12, CA.
- *R* v. *Qureshi* [2002] 1 WLR 518, CA.
- *R* v. *Mirza (Shabbir Ali)* [2004] 1 AC 1118, HL; [2002] Crim LR 921, CA.

In *Mirza* the Court of Appeal considered itself bound by both the common law rule and the operation of the Contempt of Court Act 1981. The appellants in both cases appealed further to the House of Lords (see below).

There are exceptions to the common law rule, which predominantly relate to juries influenced by matters *outside* the jury room. Perhaps the most well-known instance of this occurred in *R* v. *Young* [1995] QB 324, CA, where the Court of Appeal *allowed* evidence concerning the use of an ouija board by four jurors *during an overnight stay in a hotel*.

The Contempt of Court Act 1981, s. 8

A gap in the common law was identified in *Attorney-General* v. *New Statesman* [1981] QB 1, DC. Here, in relation to the publication of an anonymous interview with a juror, it was held that disclosure of the secrets of the jury room was *not* contrary to the common law unless it interfered with the final verdict. This gap was almost immediately filled by the Contempt of Court Act 1981.

Section 8 of the Contempt of Court Act 1981

It is a contempt to obtain, disclose or solicit any particulars of statements made, opinions expressed, arguments advanced, or votes cast by members of a jury in the course of their deliberations in any legal proceedings.

In *Young*, it was held that s. 8 applies equally to *judges* and, hence, the Court of Appeal could not investigate what happened in the jury room without committing contempt of court.

However, this was not upheld in the House of Lords appeal in *R* v. *Mirza (Shabbir Ali)* [2004] 1 AC 1118, HL – a court cannot be in contempt of itself. This was quickly followed by a new practice direction requiring judges to warn jurors to bring to their attention any concerns about jury impropriety, as later rectification may be impossible.

In *Attorney-General* v. *Scotcher* [2005] UKHL 36, the House of Lords upheld the conviction of a dissenting juror who wrote to the mother of two brothers convicted of drugs offences, thereby disclosing the jury's deliberations and advising her to bring an appeal. His intention to expose an injustice was no defence to proceedings under s. 8 of the Contempt of Court Act 1981.

Criticisms

 EXAM TIP

The jury is another potentially wide-ranging topic. Check to see if your course goes into additional detail. Essay questions may require an evaluation of advantages and disadvantages of the jury system and any possibilities for reform – some possible headings are given here, but you must also do your own further reading and thinking and form your own reasoned opinion.

Advantages?	Disadvantages?
Represents liberty against the state (often stated by way of the popular cliché, 'the lamp that shows that freedom lives')	Jurors can be intimidated, bribed or otherwise 'nobbled'

Advantages?	Disadvantages?
Involves 'ordinary' people in the processes of justice	Jurors may not be sufficiently objective
Barometer of social opinion against potential harshness of the criminal law	Jurors may be too easily influenced by counsel or the judge
Twelve people will mitigate each other's prejudices	Jury awards of damages in civil cases (in particular, libel actions) may be unfeasibly high
The only viable option?	Jurors might not understand serious or complex cases (although in such cases a preparatory hearing may be ordered to ensure that evidence is as comprehensible to a jury as possible); see also the section above on 'Trials without a jury'
	Process is costly and time consuming
	Jurors can be influenced by the media
	Jurors may find certain trials distressing
	Since jury verdicts are unexplained, it is often difficult to formulate an appeal

■ Putting it all together

Answer guidelines

See the sample question at the start of the chapter. A diagram illustrating how to structure your answer is available on the companion website.

Approaching the question

This might seem like a difficult question, since it starts with a somewhat controversial and provocative statement. You should spend some time planning the sorts of points that you might cover in your answer. Try to rephrase the question: for instance, you could imagine it as being: 'Evaluate the advantages and disadvantages of the jury system and consider whether the jury system is still the best means of adjudging guilt or innocence in Britain today.' This would give you a better idea of the points to include. ▶

Important points to include

One potential plan for tackling this essay would be as follows:

- A strong introduction setting out your approach.

- An analysis of the advantages and disadvantages of the jury system as it is today (look again at the table in the 'Criticisms' section).

- For each point, try and link back to the question in some way. For instance: 'The random selection of jurors could lead to a situation in which all jurors are white. This could potentially lead to bias against a non-white defendant and, moreover, be unrepresentative of the ethnic diversity within modern Britain.'

- Discuss the reforms on eligibility for jury service introduced by the Criminal Justice Act 2003 and whether these are more appropriate.

- Consider the proposals for trials without jury in complex fraud cases.

- Analysis of potential alternatives to the jury system.

- A concise conclusion bringing together your arguments for and against the statement.

 Make your answer stand out

In questions like this, most credit will be given for reasoned and substantiated analysis rather than a simply descriptive account. It is always important to tie each of your points back to the essay title itself. At the end of each point, look for a way in which you can refer to the question. This will demonstrate to the examiner that you are writing with the question in mind (many students do not) and that your points have relevance to the question asked and are not just abstract statements about juries. Keeping a strong focus in this way and wrapping everything up with a strong conclusion could lead to a better structured answer, which should, in turn, be reflected in its mark.

READ TO IMPRESS

Abel, R. (1988) *The Legal Profession in England and Wales*, Oxford: Basil Blackwell.

Browne-Wilkinson, N. (1999) 'The independence of the judiciary in the 1980s', *Public Law* 4.

McLachlin, B. (1994) 'The role of judges in modern Commonwealth society', *Law Quarterly Review* 260.

www.pearsoned.co.uk/lawexpress

 Go online to access more revision support including quizzes to test your knowledge, sample questions with answer guidelines, podcasts you can download, and more!

Criminal procedure

6

Revision checklist

Essential points you should know:

- [ ] How criminal proceedings are started
- [ ] The factors which influence whether a particular alleged offence will be prosecuted
- [ ] The operation of bail, how it is granted and why it may be refused
- [ ] Procedure through the magistrates' and Crown Courts
- [ ] The powers of criminal courts of appeal
- [ ] Some of the safeguards that are in place to prevent miscarriages of justice

▨ Topic map

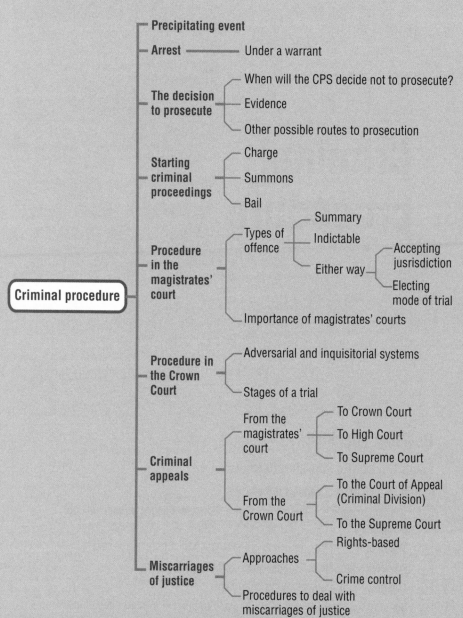

- Precipitating event
- Arrest ——— Under a warrant
- The decision to prosecute
  - When will the CPS decide not to prosecute?
  - Evidence
  - Other possible routes to prosecution
- Starting criminal proceedings
  - Charge
  - Summons
  - Bail
- Procedure in the magistrates' court
  - Types of offence
    - Summary
    - Indictable
    - Either way
      - Accepting jusrisdiction
      - Electing mode of trial
  - Importance of magistrates' courts
- Procedure in the Crown Court
  - Adversarial and inquisitorial systems
  - Stages of a trial
- Criminal appeals
  - From the magistrates' court
    - To Crown Court
    - To High Court
    - To Supreme Court
  - From the Crown Court
    - To the Court of Appeal (Criminal Division)
    - To the Supreme Court
- Miscarriages of justice
  - Approaches
    - Rights-based
    - Crime control
  - Procedures to deal with miscarriages of justice

Criminal procedure

A printable version of this topic map is available from **www.pearsoned.co.uk/lawexpress**

■ Introduction

Criminal procedure covers everything from arrest to conviction or acquittal

This chapter looks at what happens before, during and after criminal trials. It starts by looking at ways in which criminal proceedings can begin before considering whether or not any particular case will end up in court. There are many stages throughout the criminal justice process where cases might 'drop out' of the system; indeed, data from the British Crime Survey shows that for every 100 offences committed, only around three end up in court. Once a case is to be prosecuted, its route through the system will depend on a number of factors, starting with the classification of the offence in terms of its severity. We will look at the various routes through the magistrates' court and the Crown Court, considering whether there is scope for any reform of the process, before moving on to look at criminal appeals and concluding with a brief mention of some of the rules of evidence.

Essay questions on the criminal process typically attempt to test two main areas of knowledge – a substantive knowledge of the mechanics of the process itself and an informed substantiated opinion of some of the reasons behind the process. Although there are favourite essay topics that arise in this area – including matters such as mode of trial – there is almost limitless scope for variation. Some aspects of the criminal process are also immediately familiar; however, if in doubt, do not try to use your layperson's knowledge on this area – it will be immediately obvious to your examiner that your opinion is based on your views as a 'person in the street' and not as a well-informed, well-prepared law student; your marks will probably reflect this too.

Problem questions in this area could involve a fictitious scenario where you are asked to advise a worried potential defendant as to what is going to happen to him as he goes through the process and what options he might have open to him at each stage. It is important to be methodical. Use the approach set out in the flowcharts throughout this chapter and remember to keep your advice *relevant to the problem.* Don't advise your poor client on outcomes that would be entirely impossible – if he has been charged with murder, for example, there is no point in explaining the procedure for summary trial!

■ Sample question

Could you answer this question? Below is a typical problem question that could arise on this topic. Guidelines on answering the question are included at the end of the chapter, whilst a sample essay question and guidance on tackling it can be found on the companion website.

PROBLEM QUESTION

You have just received the following email from your good friend Barry:

Hi,

Hope your studies are going well. Things aren't so good here and I could really do with some help – sorry to have to ask but I know you're doing law so you might be able to explain a few things to me. I've been caught stealing from the car parts shop on the High Street – a set of neon under-car lights for my Corsa to be precise. They caught me red-handed and the police came and arrested me. I'm due to go to the magistrates' court next week and I'm petrified. I've no idea what's going to happen there, although I'm sure the jury won't like me. I don't like to ask my solicitor as he'll think I'm stupid. Can you help?

Advise Barry:

(a) what will happen at the magistrates' court;
(b) under what circumstances he could appear at the Crown Court;
(c) if so, what he could expect to happen at Crown Court.

■ Precipitating event

Before any criminal proceedings can commence, an event must happen which is observed and defined as crime, either by the victim or the public who then report the alleged offence to the police, or by the police themselves (see Figure 6.1). The police will then decide whether or not to take any further action in respect of the matter.

Once the police have decided to take further action, there are a number of possible next steps in the process, depending on the nature and circumstances of the alleged offence. These are shown in Figure 6.2.

Figure 6.1

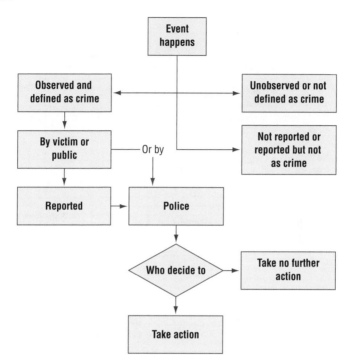

■ Arrest

Under a warrant

In order to initiate an arrest under a warrant, the police must satisfy a magistrate that the person concerned 'has, or is suspected of having, committed an offence' (s. 1 Magistrates' Courts Act 1980); then a warrant may be issued for that person's arrest. Although used quite infrequently, arrest under warrant is most commonly used when a defendant on bail fails to turn up for court; it can also be used for the arrest of suspected criminals who have fled the jurisdiction on their return to the United Kingdom.

Without a warrant

Most arrests are carried out without a warrant. As with the majority of police powers, the statutory power of arrest is provided by the Police and Criminal Evidence Act 1984 (this is usually referred to simply as 'PACE', as you will see throughout the remainder of this chapter).

Figure 6.2

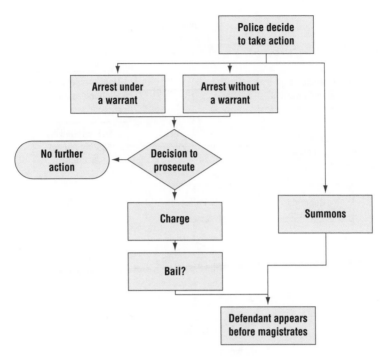

When writing an exam answer involving police powers, you will save a lot of time by abbreviating the 'Police and Criminal Evidence Act 1984' to 'PACE'. However, you should refer to it in full *the first time* that you use it in an answer, with the abbreviation that you intend to use in brackets afterwards. So, your essay might begin 'Police powers are largely governed by the Police and Criminal Evidence Act 1984 ('PACE') . . . section 24 of PACE (as amended) considers the general power of arrest . . .'

The provisions relating to powers of arrest within PACE were substituted by the Serious Organised Crime and Police Act 2005, making all classes of offence 'arrestable' if the 'necessary criteria' apply.

Section 24 of PACE (as substituted by s. 110 of the Serious Organised Crime and Police Act 2005)

1 A constable may arrest without a warrant
   (a) anyone who is about to commit an offence;
   (b) anyone who is in the act of committing an offence;
   (c) anyone whom he has reasonable grounds for suspecting to be about to commit an offence;
   (d) anyone whom he has reasonable grounds for suspecting to be committing an offence.
2 If a constable has reasonable grounds for suspecting that an offence has been committed, he may arrest without a warrant anyone whom he has reasonable grounds to suspect of being guilty of it.
3 If an offence has been committed, a constable may arrest without a warrant
   (a) anyone who is guilty of the offence;
   (b) anyone whom he has reasonable grounds for suspecting to be guilty of it.

Section 24 of PACE (as substituted) applies to *any* offence and means that the grounds for making an arrest are that a constable has reasonable grounds to believe that a person *is* committing, *has* committed or *is about to* commit an offence. However, for the arrest to be lawful, the constable must also have reasonable grounds for believing that the arrest is *necessary* for any of the criteria listed in s. 24(5) of PACE (as substituted).

Section 24(5) of PACE (as substituted by s. 110 of the Serious Organised Crime and Police Act 2005)

5 The reasons [to necessitate an arrest without a warrant] are –
   (a) to enable the name of the person in question to be ascertained (in the case where the constable does not know, and cannot readily ascertain, the person's name, or has reasonable grounds for doubting whether a name given by the person as his name is his real name);
   (b) correspondingly as regards the person's address;
   (c) to prevent the person in question –
      (i) causing physical injury to himself or any other person;
      (ii) suffering physical injury;
      (iii) causing loss of or damage to property;
      (iv) committing an offence against public decency; (subject to subsection (6) which states that section 24(5)(c)(iv) applies only where members ►

of the public going about their normal business cannot reasonably be expected to avoid the person in question);

   (v)   causing an unlawful obstruction of the highway;

(d) to protect a child or other vulnerable person from the person in question;

(e) to allow the prompt and effective investigation of the offence or of the conduct of the person in question;

(f) to prevent any prosecution for the offence from being hindered by the disappearance of the person in question.

It is not just police officers who have the power of arrest. Under certain circumstances ordinary people can arrest without a warrant – a so-called 'citizen's arrest' – the power for which is conferred by s. 24A of PACE. This is a new section that was inserted by s. 110 of the Serious Organised Crime and Police Act 2005, although the power of citizen's arrest did exist before PACE was amended. The amendments replaced a more complex array of arrest powers with a much more rationalised power whereby all offences are arrestable subject to the necessity criteria.

KEY STATUTE

Section 24A of PACE (as substituted by s. 110 of the Serious Organised Crime and Police Act 2005)

1   A person other than a constable may arrest without a warrant –
    (a) anyone who is in the act of committing an indictable offence;
    (b) anyone whom he has reasonable grounds for suspecting to be committing an indictable offence.

2   Where an indictable offence has been committed, a person other than a constable may arrest without a warrant –
    (a) anyone who is guilty of the offence;
    (b) anyone whom he has reasonable grounds for suspecting to be guilty of it.

3   But the power of summary arrest conferred by subsection (1) or (2) is exercisable only if –
    (a) the person making the arrest has reasonable grounds for believing that for any of the reasons mentioned in subsection (4) it is necessary to arrest the person in question;
    (b) it appears to the person making the arrest that it is not reasonably practicable for a constable to make it instead.

4   The reasons are to prevent the person in question –
    (a) causing physical injury to himself or any other person;
    (b) suffering physical injury;
    (c) causing loss or damage to property; or
    (d) making off before a constable can assume responsibility for him.

The provisions relating to powers of arrest are considerably simpler than before. However, you should read through the provisions of ss. 24 and 24A carefully to make sure you particularly understand the reasons to necessitate arrest by a police officer without a warrant, and arrest by a member of the public.

After arrest the police will carry out their investigations and gather evidence. If the police are unable to find sufficient evidence they will take no further action.

Responsibility for the decision to charge was moved from the police to the CPS (Crown Prosecution Service) by s. 28 of the Criminal Justice Act 2003, although the police may still charge certain minor offences. Responsibility for prosecution lies with the CPS.

📖 **REVISION NOTE**

There are certain formalities, such as the requirement to caution a suspect, with which a police officer must comply in order for an arrest to be lawful. These are governed by PACE. Moreover, once a suspect has been arrested, the police may wish to detain him for questioning and to give themselves time in which to carry out other investigations and, again, the rules which govern the detention and questioning of suspects and searches are contained within PACE (and its associated Codes of Practice). Some courses cover police powers between arrest and trial in considerable detail which is largely beyond the scope of this revision guide. You should check back through your course notes and syllabus to make sure that you know whether further revision in this area will be required for your examination.

■ The decision to prosecute

Before 1986, the decision to prosecute was primarily in the hands of the police. However, in its 1970 report, *The Prosecution Process in England and Wales*, JUSTICE (the British arm of the International Commission of Jurists) argued that the police should not take the role of prosecutor as well as investigator as they tended to commit to trying to win cases despite weak evidence, and that they would not properly consider the wider social implications of their discretion not to prosecute. In effect, JUSTICE argued that the police had too much power when it came to criminal prosecutions. This was backed up some years later in the 1981 report of the Philips Royal Commission on Criminal Justice which proposed a new State prosecuting agency, and eventually in 1986 (following the Prosecution of Offences Act 1985) the CPS came into being.

The CPS

Responsibility	The conduct of most criminal proceedings instigated by the police The decision whether or not to prosecute most alleged criminal offences
Personnel	Solicitors and barristers (see Chapter 5)
Head	Director of Public Prosecutions (the 'DPP'). The DPP must be a solicitor or barrister of at least 10 years' experience

When will the CPS decide not to prosecute?

The CPS has its own guide for Crown Prosecutors. The CPS operates a *two-stage test* in deciding whether or not to proceed with a prosecution. This comprises an *evidential* stage and a *public-interest* stage. If a case does not pass the evidential stage it must not go ahead no matter how important or serious it may be. If the evidential stage is passed, the CPS will still discontinue proceedings if it considers that the prosecution is not in the public interest.

Evidential stage	Public-interest stage
Must be sufficient evidence	Considers a range of factors in favour of and against prosecution:
	Seriousness of offence?
	Circumstances of offence?
	Circumstances of offender?
	Circumstances of victim?
Evidence must provide a 'realistic prospect' of conviction (in other words, is it more likely than not that a properly directed jury would convict the defendant on the evidence available?) (e.g. *R (on the application of Da Silva)* v. *DPP* [2006] EWHC 3204.)	
Can the evidence be used?	
Is it reliable?	

Evidence

A witness cannot present evidence to the court that was told to him by someone else – this is known as *hearsay* evidence. This rule is designed to protect against unfairness to the defendant – it hardly seems fair to present evidence from someone who cannot be cross-examined. Witnesses, therefore, may only generally present something which they perceived themselves. In practice, however, there are a number of exceptions to this general rule, including:

- business documents;
- admissions or confessions (subject to the rules about admissibility of confessions obtained in oppressive or demonstrably unreliable circumstances);
- written witness statements;
- statements that are 'spontaneous and contemporaneous' with the event (such as things said by the victim at the time of the alleged offence) – these are generically known as *res gestae*.

The defendant's previous criminal record or any communications between him and his barrister or solicitor are also generally inadmissible as evidence.

Other possible routes to prosecution

The CPS does not deal with every decision to prosecute. Very serious crimes, such as terrorist offences or alleged breaches of the Official Secrets Act, need the consent of the Attorney-General. Other authorities, such as the Inland Revenue, can also commence criminal proceedings.

Private individuals can also bring prosecutions under s. 6 of the Prosecution of Offences Act 1985. The most common example of this is a private prosecution against the police itself, although a private prosecution may be instigated where the CPS decides not to prosecute in a particular case. The CPS also has the power to take over any private prosecution, either to continue with it or to discontinue it if there is not sufficient evidence to justify the continuation of the case or if it is contrary to public interest to allow the case to proceed. Few private prosecutions are initiated but they do have an important role to play in highlighting public concern over particular issues. In April 1995, the parents of murdered teenager Stephen Lawrence initiated a private prosecution against the five men they believed were responsible for their son's death. The prosecution was unsuccessful as there was insufficient evidence to proceed against two of the defendants and the remaining three defendants were acquitted after the trial judge ruled that witness testimony that was at the heart of the prosecution case was inadmissible.

Starting criminal proceedings

A criminal prosecution can begin in one of two ways – by *charge* (following arrest) or by *summons*.

Charge

Following arrest, the defendant will be taken to a police station, charged and either released on bail to appear before the magistrates' court at the next available session, or detained in police custody and taken before the magistrates' court as soon as practicable.

Summons

Less serious offences which do not involve an arrest (such as many motoring offences) will be treated differently. The prosecution will 'lay an information' before a magistrate or magistrate's clerk; in other words, the magistrate (or clerk) will be given details of the alleged offence with a request for the issue of a summons which is then posted to the defendant's usual or last known address. The summons will require the defendant to appear before the magistrates' court at an appointed time and date.

Bail

Bail can be defined as the release of an accused from custody before trial in return for a promise that money will be paid if the accused absconds. Section 4 of the Bail Act 1976 creates a statutory right to bail before trial.

KEY STATUTE

Section 4 of the Bail Act 1976
General right to bail of accused persons and others

1   A person to whom this section applies shall be granted bail except as provided in Schedule 1 to this Act.
2   This section applies to a person who is accused of an offence when –
    (a) he appears or is brought before a magistrates' court or the Crown Court in the course of or in connection with proceedings for the offence, or
    (b) he applies to a court for bail or for a variation of the conditions of bail in connection with the proceedings.

This subsection does not apply with respect to proceedings on or after a person's conviction of the offence.

There is, therefore, a general right to (or at least a presumption in favour of) bail, and a person arrested and charged with an offence for which he could not be imprisoned must generally be released on bail unless an exception in Schedule 1 applies. Schedule 1 is divided into two sections dealing with:

- offences punishable by imprisonment (Schedule 1(I));

- offences not punishable by imprisonment (Schedule 1(II)).

There is a balancing exercise to be carried out, between the protection of the public and the assurance that the defendant will appear in court on the one hand, and the presumption of innocence and the avoidance of unnecessary public expenditure on the other.

This general right does not apply to bail after conviction (pending sentence or appeal).

KEY STATUTE

Schedule 1(I) of the Bail Act 1976

The defendant need not be granted bail if the court is satisfied that there are substantial grounds for believing that the defendant, if released on bail (whether subject to conditions or not) would –

(a)   fail to surrender to custody, OR
(b)   commit an offence while on bail, OR
(c)   interfere with witnesses or otherwise obstruct the course of justice, whether in relation to himself or any other person.

In deciding whether or not to grant bail, the magistrates will consider a number of factors (see Figure 6.3), including:

- the severity of the offence – the more serious the offence, the greater the likelihood that the defendant will abscond;

- the character and any previous criminal record of the defendant;

- the defendant's background, upbringing, education and employment history;

- the type of person that the defendant mixes with;

- any community ties – factors that 'cement' the defendant to his present place (family, children at school, mortgage, job);

- the strength of evidence – the stronger the case, the greater the likelihood of absconding.

For less serious offences, not punishable by imprisonment, the exceptions to the right to bail are weaker. Bail is generally granted in these cases.

Under s. 25 of the Criminal Justice and Public Order Act 1994 (as amended), a person charged with murder, manslaughter or rape, or attempted murder or rape, who has previously been convicted and imprisoned (or found not guilty by reason of insanity) for any of these offences, is not to be granted bail unless there are exceptional circumstances to justify it. The original form of s. 25 stated 'shall not be granted bail' but was found to breach Article 5 (right to liberty and security of the person) of the European Convention on Human Rights (*CC* v. *UK* [1999] Crim LR 228, ECtHR).

Parts of the Coroners and Justice Act 2009, which made changes to the Bail Act 1976, came into force on 1 February 2010. Reflecting government policy that the safety of the public

Figure 6.3

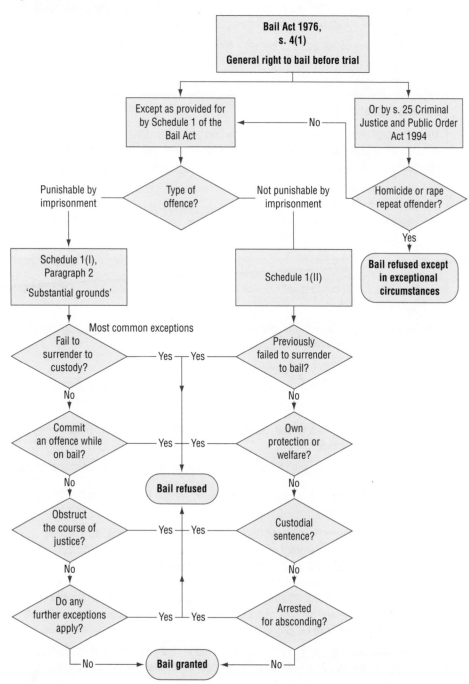

should be the guiding principle, these underline the need for a cautious approach where defendants pose a risk of harm. The new provisions focus primarily on bail for defendants charged with murder:

- bail in such cases can be considered only by a judge of the Crown Court (s. 115);
- a defendant charged with murder may not be granted bail unless the court is of the opinion that there is no significant risk of him committing an offence that would be likely to cause injury (s. 114(2)).

The Act also introduces a new consideration affecting bail decisions in respect of any indictable offence punishable by imprisonment. In such cases, where the court is satisfied that there are substantial grounds for believing the defendant would commit further offences if bailed, it must have regard to the risk that such further offending would be likely to cause injury (s. 114(3)).

📖 **REVISION NOTE**

You may have noticed that there are a number of stages in the criminal justice process in which various parties can exercise their discretion. These include:

- police – deciding whether to arrest or request a summons;
- police – deciding whether they have sufficient evidence to refer a case to the CPS;
- CPS – deciding whether to charge or prosecute (on evidential and/or public-interest grounds);
- magistrates – deciding whether to issue a warrant for arrest or a summons;
- magistrates – deciding whether or not to grant bail.

A tricky exam question might involve asking you to discuss the exercise of discretion throughout the criminal justice process. Although you might think this too difficult, if you really know your subject matter you should be able to put together a well-structured answer that will impress the examiner. This sort of open-ended question invites the unwary or ill-prepared to waffle on with no meaningful structure or, even worse, no real substance. A good answer to a question that others will do badly will really shine out.

■ Procedure in the magistrates' court

📖 **REVISION NOTE**

It is important to understand the role of the magistrates and the magistrates' court when revising the procedure. These topics are dealt with in Chapter 5 which looks at the personnel of the legal system.

The procedure followed at the magistrates' court will depend on the nature of the alleged criminal offence in question. Criminal offences are divided into three categories as follows:

Summary offences	Summary offences can only be tried in the magistrates' court.
	Summary offences are all defined by statute. The definition is negative – that is, if the statute does not state a penalty for conviction on indictment then the offence is a summary one. For example, s. 89(1) of the Police Act 1996 states that:
	any person who assaults a constable in the execution of his duty . . . shall be guilty of an offence and liable on summary conviction to imprisonment for a term not exceeding six months or to a fine not exceeding the amount at level 5 on the standard scale, or to both.
	As s. 89(1) does not state what penalty would be applied on conviction on indictment, this indicates that this offence is summary only. Some summary offences are relatively serious – assaulting a police officer, drink driving.
Offences triable only on indictment (indictable offences)	Indictable offences can only be tried in the Crown Court (s. 51, Crime and Disorder Act 1998).
	All common law offences are indictable, as well as the more serious statutory offences – also known as 'indictable' offences – such as rape, robbery and murder.
Offences 'triable either way'	Statutory offences may be triable on indictment only but are more usually triable either way, meaning that they may be heard either in the magistrates' court or at Crown Court.
	Offences which are triable either way can be identified in two ways:
	■ the statute creating them may state a maximum penalty both for summary conviction and for conviction upon indictment; ■ offences which are triable either way are listed in s. 17 and Schedule 1 of the Magistrates' Courts Act 1980.
	Offences which are triable either way tend to represent either a middle tier of seriousness, such as making off without payment contrary to s. 3 of the Theft Act 1978, or are those in which the seriousness of the offence is contingent upon its particular circumstances, such as theft or criminal damage (the seriousness of these will clearly depend on the value of the property stolen or the amount of damage caused). Other examples include handling stolen goods, burglary, assault occasioning actual bodily harm ('ABH') and indecent assault.

The next steps in the process are best illustrated by way of a diagram (see Figure 6.4).

Figure 6.4

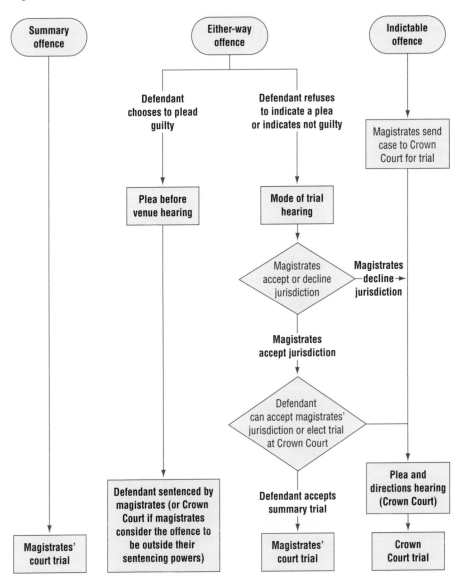

Summary offences

Summary offences, as indicated in the table above, must be dealt with by the magistrates' court. The defendant will make a plea of guilty or not guilty and if convicted will be sentenced by the magistrates. If defendants fail to attend without good cause, they may be tried, convicted and sentenced in their absence (s. 54, Criminal Justice and Immigration Act 2008).

Indictable offences

Under procedures introduced by s. 51 of the Crime and Disorder Act 1998, the magistrates must send cases triable on indictment immediately to the Crown Court for trial.

A plea and case management hearing will be held before Crown Court trial per the Criminal Procedure Rules 2005. This is generally a very brief exercise at which the defendant will enter a plea and, if it is not guilty, the court will give directions as to the preparations that are to be made by each side before the trial. If the plea is guilty, then the judge will invite the defendant to make a '*plea in mitigation*' – basically a statement designed to encourage the judge towards leniency in sentencing – before proceeding to sentencing whenever possible.

Offences triable either way

The procedure for either-way offences is more complex. The stages of this are set out in the table below. Work through the procedure flowchart as you read the table below. Make sure you understand the various routes through the process and what decides which route a particular case will take.

Stages of a magistrates' court trial

Stage	Comment
The clerk to the magistrates asks the defendant if he wishes to indicate how he intends to plea if the matter proceeds to trial	The defendant does not have to indicate any plea at all. However, if he indicates a plea of guilty, then the court will proceed to sentencing (a 'plea before venue' hearing). If he indicates a plea of not guilty, or declines to indicate any plea, then the court moves to the mode of trial procedure.
Mode of trial hearing – magistrates accept or decline jurisdiction	The magistrates will either decide to accept jurisdiction and deal with the case themselves or decide that the case is suitable for Crown Court trial. This will be done according to s. 19 of the Magistrates' Court Act 1980 and the Mode of Trial Guidelines (see below).

Stage	Comment
Mode of trial hearing – defendant can accept the magistrates' jurisdiction or elect trial at Crown Court	If the magistrates agree to accept jurisdiction, the accused nonetheless has the right to refuse to be tried by them and may instead opt for Crown Court trial. This 'right to elect' trial by jury is a controversial feature of the criminal justice system (see below). If the defendant opts for Crown Court trial, the next stage will be a plea and directions hearing as for an indictable offence (see above) before full Crown Court trial.
Sentencing – do the magistrates consider the offence to be within their sentencing powers?	If the magistrates consider that the punishment for the offence falls within their powers, they will pass sentence. If they consider that the offence is deserving of a punishment greater than they can impose, then they may refer the case to the Crown Court for sentencing. The maximum penalty which can currently be imposed by the magistrates' court is six months' imprisonment and/or a fine of £5,000 for any one offence triable either way. For any two or more offences the maximum is 12 months' imprisonment and/or a fine of £5,000.

Factors considered by magistrates when deciding whether to accept jurisdiction

KEY STATUTE

Section 19 of the Magistrates' Court Act 1980

1   The court shall consider whether, having regard to the matters mentioned in subsection (3) below, and any representations made by the prosecutor or the accused, the offence appears to the court to be more suitable for summary trial or trial on indictment.

Section 19(3)

3   The matters to which the court is to have regard under subsection (1) above are the nature of the case; whether the circumstances make the offence one of serious character; whether the punishment which a magistrates' court would have power to inflict for it would be adequate and any other circumstances which appear to the court to make it more suitable for the offence to be tried in one way rather than the other.

The statutory guidance given to magistrates to assist them to determine mode of trial in relation to either-way offences is supplemented by the *Mode of Trial Guidelines* which reiterate the provisions of s. 19 and highlight the following considerations:

- the court should never make its decision on the grounds of convenience or expedition;
- the court should assume for the purposes of determining mode of trial that the prosecution version of the facts is correct (in other words, the decision as regards mode of trial is based on the 'worst case scenario' for the defendant);
- cases involving complex facts or difficult questions of law should be considered for remittal to Crown Court;
- in general, either-way offences should be tried summarily unless one or more of a list of stated features (listed for each separate offence) is present *and* the court considers its sentencing powers will be inadequate;
- the court should remember it has the power to remit the case to Crown Court for sentencing if, after hearing all the evidence and convicting the defendant, it finds that the seriousness of the case exceeds its maximum sentencing powers.

A defendant's right to elect mode of trial – a controversial feature?

✎ EXAM TIP

An understanding of procedure is, of course, vital to any law student. However, the ability to reflect critically on why any aspect of the law exists in the form that it does and express a reasoned analysis of the pros and cons is a skill that will set you apart from the average student. This skill will almost inevitably be tested by way of an essay question, which will usually be done very badly by those who understand *what* the law (or in this case, procedure) is and better by those who can express a measured and balanced view as to *why* it is, *and how it might be improved.* This sort of question will give you the opportunity to make 'clever' points which are always rewarded by better marks.

The Royal Commission Report on the Criminal Justice System (1993) (often referred to as the 'Runciman Commission') recommended, controversially, that the right to elect trial by jury should be removed in certain circumstances:

Circumstances	Proposed outcome
CPS and defendant agree that the case is suitable for summary trial	Trial proceeds in magistrates' court
CPS and defendant agree that the case should be tried on indictment	Case is sent for Crown Court trial
Defendant does not agree with CPS's proposal on mode of trial	Magistrates decide whether they should try the case or send it to the Crown Court

Two later attempts to implement the Runciman proposals failed in the House of Lords.

Criminal Justice (Mode of Trial) Bill (2000)	Proposed the removal of the right of a defendant pleading not guilty to elect Crown Court trial, even if the magistrates consider the case to be suitable for summary trial. In particular, the Bill sought to protect the rights of individuals with good reputations. This was heavily criticised by civil liberties organisations and the legal profession.
Criminal Justice (Mode of Trial) (No. 2) Bill (2000)	The Bill was reintroduced with the 'good reputations' provisions removed – it now stated that no personal characteristic of the accused (including reputation) should be taken into account by the magistrates in determining mode of trial.

Finally, Lord Justice Auld's review of the criminal courts identified the essence of the problem as follows. When magistrates decline jurisdiction, they believe that the offence in question is at the top end of their scale of seriousness. When the case appears in the Crown Court, it is at the lower end of that court's scale of seriousness. Quite often the Crown Court then imposes a sentence (at the end of a much more expensive exercise – the cost of a Crown Court trial is around £14,000) which would have been within the sentencing powers of the magistrates. Furthermore, defendants often strategically elect Crown Court trial. Since this is more expensive, there is a greater likelihood that the case will be dropped by the CPS. The report concluded that the categories of summary and indictable offences should be reviewed to see if they need to be expanded (and thus reduce the number of either-way offences); finally, for the remaining either-way offences, a separate panel would decide mode of trial based on the circumstances, the complexity of the facts and the complexity of the law.

How important are magistrates' courts?

	Proportion of cases	Proportion pleading not guilty	Acquittal rate*	Cost of trial
Magistrates' court	98%	82%	25%	£1,500
Crown Court	2%	65%	40%	£13,500

*Acquittal rate as a percentage of contested trials

- Trial by jury is perceived by the public to be the cornerstone of the criminal justice system, yet surprisingly few cases are tried in the Crown Court.
- Magistrates are responsible for the dispensation of justice in the vast majority of cases, dealing with 1,390,000 offenders in 1998.
- There is also a perception that magistrates deal with only trivial cases: however, prison statistics show that of the 91,282 sentenced to imprisonment in 1998, 54% (48,910) were sentenced by magistrates.

Therefore, in magistrates' courts:

- the vast majority (98%) of criminal cases are heard by magistrates;
- more than four-fifths of those cases involve guilty pleas by the defendant;
- only one-quarter of those who plead not guilty are acquitted;
- contested trials are less frequent and significantly cheaper in magistrates' courts.

However, in the Crown Court:

- only 2% of criminal cases are heard by judge and jury;
- of those cases, two-thirds plead not guilty thus necessitating a full jury trial;
- there is a significantly higher chance of acquittal on a not-guilty plea;
- contested trials are more frequent (two out of three cases) and significantly more costly.

 Make your answer stand out

Allowing the defendant to elect mode of trial remains one of the most controversial elements of criminal procedure and one which has been recommended to be abolished or modified on many occasions. The full Auld Report can be found online at: http://www.criminal-courts-review.org.uk/summary.htm#top

■ Procedure in the Crown Court

Adversarial and inquisitorial systems

Court cases under the English legal system are adversarial rather than inquisitorial. The distinction can be clearly seen when considering criminal cases.

Adversarial system	Inquisitorial system
Is the person charged with a particular offence guilty of that offence as charged?	Has a crime been committed? If so, by whom?

Although it is common to hear that most continental civil law systems are inquisitorial, most *European* civil law systems have incorporated some adversarial elements to meet their obligations under the European Convention on Human Rights.

The stages of a trial

The basic stages of a Crown Court trial can be depicted as in Figure 6.5.

As you did with the procedure in the magistrates' court, work through the flowchart as you read the table that follows.

Stage	Comment
Commencement of the trial	The judge enters the courtroom. The defendant is then called into the dock by the clerk of the court who then confirms his identity, reads out the charge against him and confirms the defendant's plea.
The jury	If the defendant has pleaded not guilty, 12 people are chosen at random by the clerk of the court from the pool of individuals called for jury service. The jury is then sworn in and informed of the charge against the defendant.
Case for the prosecution – opening speech	Counsel for the prosecution will begin by outlining the case against the defendant, summarising the evidence that he will use and explaining the various witnesses he will call (with some indication of what he thinks they will say). He will also inform the jury of the *burden* and *standard* of proof (see below).

▶

Figure 6.5

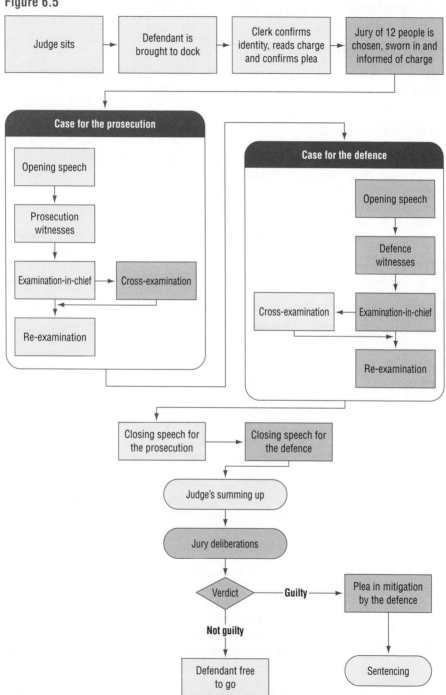

Stage	Comment
Case for the prosecution	The first witness is examined by counsel for the prosecution (known as examination-in-chief). He may not ask leading questions (questions which suggest an answer or make an assumption about something factual that has not been proved). The witness is then cross-examined by counsel for the defence (who may ask leading questions). Counsel for the prosecution is allowed (if he wishes) to re-examine the witness (in order to try and redress any weaknesses in his case introduced as a result of cross-examination).
Case for the defence – no case to answer	Counsel for the defence may attempt to persuade the judge that no reasonable jury could convict the defendant on the basis of the evidence that the prosecution has put forward. This legal argument will be done without the jury present. If the judge agrees, he will call in the jury and direct them to acquit the defendant.
Case for the defence	Counsel for the defence will make an opening speech in the same way as the prosecution. He will call defence witnesses who will be examined-in-chief, cross-examined by the prosecution and re-examined by the defence.
The judge	The judge may intervene at any stage to ask questions.
Closing speeches	Prosecution and defence will summarise the main points of their cases, concentrating on the strengths and discounting any weaknesses.
Summing up by the judge	The judge's summing up will explain to the jury the main points of the *law* in relation to the case and remind them that it is their job to decide **questions of *fact***.
Jury deliberations	The jury will elect a foreman from among themselves and then deliberate in private, attempting to reach a unanimous verdict. If they can, they return to the court and the foreman announces their verdict. If not the judge may direct them that a majority verdict of 11 to 1 or 10 to 2 may be acceptable.
Verdict	The jury announces whether they find the defendant guilty or not guilty. If not guilty, the defendant is free to go. If guilty, the prosecution will inform the court of the defendant's criminal record (if any). ▶

Stage	Comment
Plea in mitigation	Counsel for the defence will attempt to persuade the judge to be lenient when sentencing, stressing relevant points of the defendant's background and circumstances.
Sentencing	The judge may choose to adjourn for pre-sentence reports. If not, the judge will proceed to pass sentence, bearing in mind any parameters imposed by legislation. This could be a combination of fine, custodial sentence (imprisonment) and/or community sentences (such as a community rehabilitation order – formerly known as probation – or a community punishment order – previously called a community service order.

KEY DEFINITIONS: Burden of proof and standard of proof

The terms 'burden' and 'standard' of proof are often confused. The burden of proof refers to the side who has to establish proof. The standard of proof is the required threshold that the proof needs to reach. In a criminal case the burden lies on the *prosecution* and the standard of proof is *beyond reasonable doubt*. In other words, it is for the prosecution to prove the defendant's guilt beyond reasonable doubt – the defendant is therefore innocent until proven guilty with no reasonable doubt in the mind of the jury.

📖 REVISION NOTE

You may wish to revise your knowledge of the jury and criticisms of the jury system at this stage. These topics are dealt with in Chapter 5 which looks at the personnel of the legal system.

■ The criminal appeals system

Appeals from the magistrates' court after summary trial

The various routes of appeal after summary trial in the magistrates' court are set out in Figure 6.6.

Figure 6.6

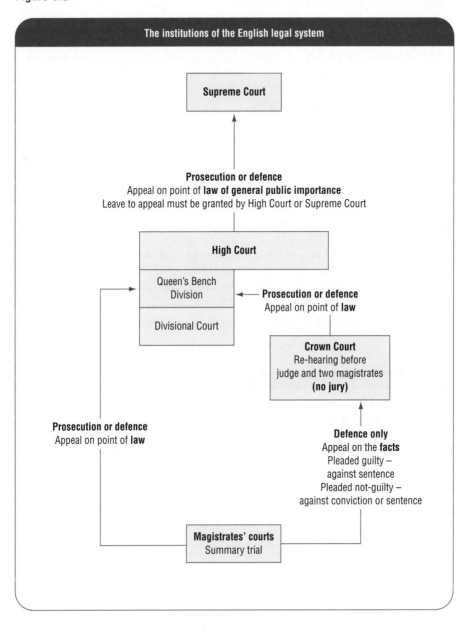

Appeals to the Crown Court

The defendant has a right to appeal to the Crown Court against conviction or sentence or both (s. 108 of the Magistrates' Courts Act 1980). This is an appeal on the *facts*. If the defendant pleaded not guilty at first instance and is appealing against conviction there will be a complete re-hearing of the case in the Crown Court before a judge and two to four magistrates. Witnesses may be called, but there will be *no jury*. If the defendant is appealing against sentence, no witnesses are called.

The Crown Court can:

- affirm, reverse or amend the decision of the magistrates;
- vary sentence (within the sentencing powers of the magistrates) – this can include increasing the sentence.

Appeals to the High Court

The prosecution or defence may appeal to the Divisional Court of the High Court (Queen's Bench Division) either directly against the decision of the magistrates' court or as a result of any appeal in the Crown Court (s. 111 of the Magistrates' Courts Act 1980). Appeals to the High Court can only be brought on matters of *law*.

The procedure for bringing the appeal to the High Court is known as **appeal by way of case stated**.

KEY DEFINITION: Appeal by way of case stated

Appeal by way of case stated is a procedure whereby the court against whose decision the appeal is being raised prepares a document for the High Court with a formal request for the opinion of the High Court on whether it was correct in the law and in the application of the law to the facts of that particular case (in other words, the court 'states its case' for consideration by the High Court).

The case document will contain the proven facts, the relevant law as understood by the court and the reasons for its decision (in other words, how it applied its understanding of the law to the proven facts in order to reach its conclusion).

The High Court can:

- remit the case to the magistrates' court with its opinion;
- affirm, reverse or amend the decision of the magistrates;
- direct the magistrates to convict or acquit the appellant;
- make such other orders as it thinks fit.

Appeal to the High Court (Queen's Bench Division) on a matter of law after acquittal following summary trial in the magistrates' court is the only general opportunity that the prosecution has to appeal following an acquittal. This right of appeal does not arise after acquittal by a jury in the Crown Court – unless the acquittal is 'tainted' (see the section on miscarriages of justice later in this chapter).

Appeals to the Supreme Court

There is a further right to appeal on a point of law from the High Court to the Supreme Court which is available to both prosecution and defence if:

- the High Court certifies that the point of law concerned is of general public importance; and
- leave (permission) to appeal is granted by the Supreme Court or the High Court.

(Section 1 of the Administration of Justice Act 1960 as amended by the Access to Justice Act 1999 and the Constitutional Reform Act 2005.)

Appeals from the Crown Court after trial on indictment
Appeals to the Court of Appeal (Criminal Division)

Refer to Figure 6.7.

The defence may appeal against conviction or sentence to the Court of Appeal (Criminal Division) if it obtains either:

- a certificate from the trial judge that the case is fit for appeal; or
- leave to appeal from the Court of Appeal (Criminal Division).

(Section 1(2) of the Criminal Appeal Act 1968 as substituted by the Criminal Appeal Act 1995.)

Appeal against sentence is not, however, available for offences whose sentence is fixed by law (the most common example of this is murder, which carries a mandatory sentence on conviction of life imprisonment) (s. 9 of the Criminal Appeal Act 1968 – but see *R* (*on the application of Lichniak*) v. *Secretary of State for the Home Department* [2002] QB 296, DC, where leave to appeal was granted in order for the Court of Appeal to investigate whether the mandatory life sentence for murder was incompatible with the European Convention on Human Rights; this was held not to be the case and indeed later affirmed by the House of Lords ([2003] 1 AC 903, HL).

In appeals against conviction the Court of Appeal may hear witness evidence; however, in practice, this is rare, since most appeals against conviction are founded on alleged errors or inadequacies in the summing up of the trial judge and his directions to the jury before they retire to consider their verdict.

Under s. 36 of the Criminal Justice Act 1972, the Attorney-General may, following an **acquittal on indictment**, refer a point of law to the Court of Appeal.

Figure 6.7

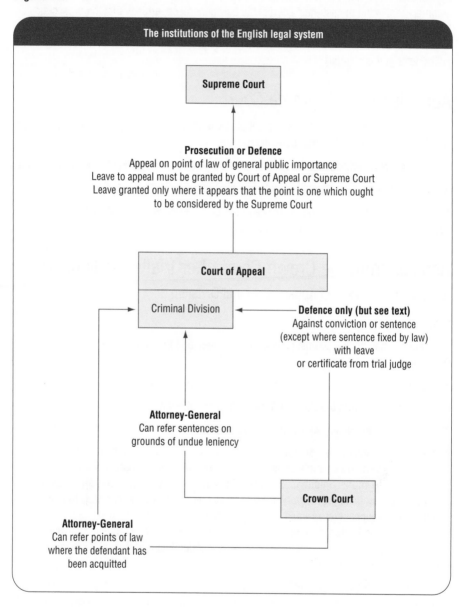

The institutions of the English legal system

Supreme Court

Prosecution or Defence
Appeal on point of law of general public importance
Leave to appeal must be granted by Court of Appeal or Supreme Court
Leave granted only where it appears that the point is one which ought
to be considered by the Supreme Court

Court of Appeal

Criminal Division

Defence only (but see text)
Against conviction or sentence
(except where sentence fixed by law)
with leave
or certificate from trial judge

Attorney-General
Can refer sentences on
grounds of undue leniency

Crown Court

Attorney-General
Can refer points of law
where the defendant has
been acquitted

! Don't be tempted to . . .

The power to refer a point of law to the Court of Appeal (Criminal Division) following an acquittal on indictment is often wrongly described as the prosecution's right to appeal against that acquittal. This is not so. Even if the Court of Appeal decides that the Crown Court erred in law, it will have no effect on the defendant who will remain acquitted.

Under s. 36 of the Criminal Justice Act 1988, the Attorney-General can also refer a case to the Court of Appeal if he considers that the sentence imposed by the Crown Court was too lenient. Here the Court of Appeal can decide to increase or decrease the actual sentence imposed.

The powers of the Court of Appeal are different for an Attorney-General's reference concerning unduly lenient sentencing (under s. 36 of the 1988 Act) compared to a reference on a point of law following acquittal (under s. 36 of the 1972 Act). Whereas the decision of the Court of Appeal in relation to an Attorney-General's reference under s. 36 of the 1972 Act does not affect the outcome of any individual case, the decision in relation to sentencing under s. 36 of the 1988 Act *does* affect the situation of the individual defendant (who may find his sentence increased or decreased as a result).

The Criminal Justice Act 2003 also allows the prosecution to appeal to the Court of Appeal in trials on indictment, where there is a ruling which terminates the prosecution case (such as 'no case to answer'). Leave to appeal must be obtained from the trial judge or the Court of Appeal. If leave is refused, the defendant must be acquitted.

📖 REVISION NOTE

The Court of Appeal also has a quasi-appellate jurisdiction by virtue of s. 9 of the Criminal Appeal Act 1995 which was designed to provide a means of correcting so-called 'miscarriages of justice'. This power will be covered in the later section of this chapter dealing with miscarriages of justice.

Appeals to the Supreme Court

The prosecution or defence may appeal on a matter of law from the Court of Appeal (Criminal Division) to the Supreme Court provided that:

■ the Court of Appeal certifies that a point of law of general public importance is involved; and

- leave to appeal is granted by either the Court of Appeal or the Supreme Court. This leave will only be granted if either the Court of Appeal or the Supreme Court considers that the point is one which ought to be considered by the Supreme Court.

(Section 33 of the Criminal Appeal Act 1968 as amended by Constitutional Reform Act 2005.)

Miscarriages of justice

What is a **miscarriage of justice**?

The dictionary defines a 'miscarriage' as the *failure to reach an intended destination or goal.*

KEY DEFINITION: Miscarriage of justice

One definition of a miscarriage of justice is *failure to attain the desired end result of justice.*

This, of course, will depend on what you believe the 'desired end result of justice' to be. There are competing views on this matter which will provide different definitions, as you will see.

! Don't be tempted to . . .

Most people think of a miscarriage of justice as a situation whereby an individual or individuals have been wrongly convicted. Famous cases in relatively recent times include the 'Guildford Four', the 'Birmingham Six', the 'Maguire Seven' and the 'Cardiff Three'. However, bearing in mind the definition above, the *prosecution* could also be the victim of a miscarriage of justice. As the prosecution in a criminal case represents the state, a perverse failure to convict is not only a miscarriage against the prosecution but arguably a miscarriage against the wider public interest – since the prosecution is representative of that public interest. In *R* v. *Mirza* [2004] 1 AC 1118, HL, Lord Hobhouse stated:

It is fundamentally wrong to use the phrase 'miscarriage of justice' selectively as if it only related to perverse convictions . . . A failure to convict a defendant whose guilt has been proved is a breach of the social contract between the state and its citizens. It is a failure of the state to provide to citizens the protection to which they are entitled against the criminal activities of others.

Approaches to criminal justice

Rights-based approach

There are different views on the roles of the criminal justice process. Sir William Blackstone (1765) famously stated that '*It is better to let ten guilty men go free than to wrongly incarcerate one innocent man*'. This statement fundamentally encapsulates a *rights-based* approach to criminal justice, leading to a definition of miscarriage of justice as something *that occurs whenever suspects or defendants or convicts are treated by the State in breach of their rights.*

Points to note as a result of this approach are:

- the meaning of miscarriage is not confined to miscarriages in court or the penal system: miscarriages can arise on the street in the unjust exercise of police powers;

- miscarriages can be institutionalised within laws as well as ensuing from failures in the application of laws;

- miscarriages must involve a shortcoming for which there is a degree of State responsibility;

- justice and failures of justice must be defined with respect to rights.

Crime-control approach

However, there are those who adopt a *crime-control* approach to the criminal justice system. In 1988 Lord Denning stated that '*wrongfully convicted prisoners should stay in jail rather than be freed and risk a loss of public confidence in the law*'.

Proponents of this model believe that:

- effective and efficient control and punishment of crime will minimise the violations of the rights of victims and maximise the deterrent effect of the criminal justice system;

- mistakes in the process can be tolerated as long as the individual is factually 'guilty' and as long as the failings do not undermine public confidence;

- rightful treatment of the accused is not of paramount importance.

📖 **REVISION NOTE**

Some courses cover more theory concerning the role and purpose of the criminal justice system than is covered here. Check your course syllabus to see if you need to do some further revision in this area.

Procedures to deal with miscarriages of justice

There are various statutory provisions designed to deal with miscarriages of justice. The procedures will depend on whether the miscarriage has been suffered by the prosecution or the defendant.

Procedures open to the prosecution

- Attorney-General's Reference under s. 36 of the Criminal Justice Act 1972 on a point of law (see above); this is largely academic as the decision of the Court of Appeal will not affect the defendant.

- Attorney-General's Reference under s. 36 of the Criminal Justice Act 1988 against unduly lenient sentencing.

- 'Tainted acquittals' (those where jurors or witnesses have been intimidated, threatened, subjected to violence or bribed to acquit or withhold incriminating evidence) can be quashed under certain circumstances under s. 54 of the Criminal Procedure and Investigations Act 1996.

- Finally, the Criminal Justice Act 2003 allows, under special circumstances, the application for retrial of serious offences and the exercise of a right of appeal against rulings by a Crown Court judge during a trial (for example, see R v. D [2007] 1 WLR 1657, CA).

Procedures open to the defendant

- Section 2(1) of the Criminal Appeal Act 1968 (as amended by the Criminal Appeal Act 1995) allows appeals to the Court of Appeal for 'unsafe' convictions.

- The Criminal Cases Review Commission can refer *at any time* the conviction, sentence or both (except for sentences fixed by law) of anyone convicted in the Crown Court to the Court of Appeal (s. 9, Criminal Appeal Act 1995); or the conviction, sentence or both of anyone convicted in the magistrates' court to the Crown Court (s. 11, Criminal Appeal Act 1995). References will only be made if:

  □ an appeal has been decided or leave to appeal has been refused; and

  □ there is a real possibility that a conviction would be overturned or a sentence not upheld because of evidence or argument not raised at the trial or appeal.

- The Home Secretary can exercise the royal prerogative of mercy over wrongful convictions. He may issue a *free pardon* to relieve the defendant of all punishment and penalty (but the conviction still stands; it may only be quashed by the Court of Appeal); a *partial* or *conditional pardon* or a *posthumous pardon* (a good example of this is the case of Derek Bentley – see R v. *Secretary of State for the Home Department, ex parte Bentley* [1994] QB 349, DC; R v. *Bentley (Derek William)* (*Deceased*) [2001] 1 Cr App R 21, CA).

■ Putting it all together

Answer guidelines

See the sample question at the start of the chapter. A diagram illustrating how to structure your answer is available on the companion website.

Approaching the question

This question requires you to demonstrate your knowledge of criminal court procedure. You should look back at Figures 6.4 and 6.5 for an overview of the magistrates' court and Crown Court procedures.

Important points to include

- It is important to identify the nature of the offence in question. Since Barry is on trial for theft (he says that he was caught stealing), we know that it is a triable either-way offence. Therefore, any discussion of summary or indictable offences would be irrelevant.

- Be methodical when working through the flowcharts and make a note of the various situations in which Barry could end up at Crown Court – if the magistrates choose, if he chooses or if he is referred there for sentencing.

- The final part of the question involves a description of the procedure at Crown Court. Remember that this will be different, depending on the reason that Barry finds himself there. If he is just there for sentencing, that will be all that happens. If he is there for the main trial for his alleged offence, you will need to go through the necessary steps – prosecution first, then defence, summing up, jury deliberation, verdict and sentencing.

 Make your answer stand out

With a question such as this, what you choose to leave out is just as important as what you include. It is important to stay focused and not include irrelevant information. Remember you have been asked to advise Barry on the circumstances *of his particular case*. What's more, by concentrating on irrelevancies, not only will you be losing marks, but losing valuable time as well. The best answers will stick to a clear structure and continually relate back to the question. Make sure you keep your advice pertinent to Barry.

▶

READ TO IMPRESS

Carlen, P. (1976) *Magistrates' Justice*, Oxford: Martin Robertson.

Moxon, D. and C. Hedderman (1994) 'Mode of trial decisions and sentencing differences between courts', 33(2) *Howard Journal of Criminal Justice* 97.

Walker, C. and K. Starmer (1999) *Miscarriages of Justice: A Review of Justice in Error*, London: Blackstone Press.

www.pearsoned.co.uk/lawexpress

Go online to access more revision support including quizzes to test your knowledge, sample questions with answer guidelines, podcasts you can download, and more!

Civil procedure

7

Revision checklist

Essential points you should know:

- [ ] An overview of the historical background to the civil procedure reforms in the 1990s
- [ ] How the Civil Procedure Rules operate in relation to civil litigation
- [ ] The different 'tracks' which a case may take through the civil courts
- [ ] Different means of alternative dispute resolution

■ Topic map

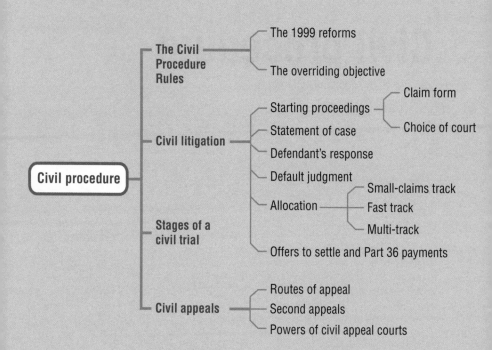

■ Introduction

Civil procedure deals with disputes between individuals

This chapter deals with various aspects of civil procedure. For revision purposes, we will begin by looking back at the civil law reforms which were introduced in the late 1990s and how these ultimately led to the introduction of the Civil Procedure Rules which are in force today. We will then review the ways in which the various civil rules apply to the most commonly encountered aspects of civil litigation, from the commencement of proceedings through to trial. This will be followed by considering the stages of a civil trial and the routes of appeal that can arise.

ASSESSMENT ADVICE

Essay questions on civil procedure can require you to understand not only the rules or procedures in question, but also some of the reasoning behind the introduction of the Civil Procedure Rules. The ability to assess critically these aspects of civil procedure will particularly help your essay stand out.

Problem questions on civil procedure can often involve applying a number of the Civil Procedure Rules to a (usually) fictitious scenario. Examiners may try to trick the unwary into discussing the wrong 'track' through the courts. You should know that there are three potential routes through the civil courts, which will usually depend on the value of the overall claim and the value for any personal injuries. Make sure that you do not confuse the two in the stress of an examination and allocate your case to the wrong track. As with any problem question, you must keep your advice relevant to the situation; there is nothing to be gained by writing all you know about small claims procedure if the claimant is suing for a million pounds.

■ Sample question

Could you answer this question? Below is a typical problem question that could arise on this topic. Guidelines on answering the question are included at the end of the chapter, whilst a sample essay question and guidance on tackling it can be found on the companion website.

PROBLEM QUESTION

Sue was driving on her way to work last Monday. James was driving his white van in the opposite direction. His local football team had won 5–1 at the weekend and he was keen to hear the match report. While he was trying to tune his radio in to get better reception he drifted towards Sue's side of the road. Sue swerved to avoid his van, ran off the road and into the side of a skip. Sue suffered a slight whiplash injury in the accident as well as badly damaging her car. The car repairs are estimated to cost £6,000 and Sue believes she should also get around £750 compensation for her injury. Her doctor has produced a medical report which was sent to her insurers along with her claim form.

Advise Sue of the likely sequence of events that will follow her claim against James. How would your answer differ (if at all) if:

(a) the car repair was estimated at £2,000;
(b) her injuries were more severe and Sue sought £3,000 compensation;
(c) her brand new car, costing £28,000, was written off?

📖 REVISION NOTE

The civil jurisdictions of the courts are dealt with in Chapter 3. Since civil procedure takes place in civil courts, you should make sure you are comfortable with the functions of each of the courts.

◼ The Civil Procedure Rules (CPR)

The 1999 reform

Prior to 1999, the civil justice system was dogged by problems of cost, delay and complexity. In response to this, in 1994 the Lord Chancellor (Lord Mackay of Clashfern) appointed Lord Woolf (a Lord of Appeal at the time, but most recently Lord Chief Justice until his retirement on 1 October 2005) to undertake an inquiry. His 1996 report *Access to Justice: final report to the Lord Chancellor on the civil justice system in England and Wales* contained around 300 recommendations for a significantly different approach to civil procedure, representing a 'new landscape' for civil litigation.

If you need to comment on the historical background to civil procedure in an examination, the 1996 report is commonly referred to as the 'Woolf Report' after its author; strictly speaking, its correct title is *Access to Justice*. Although the 'Woolf Report' would demonstrate awareness in an examination, the use of *Access to Justice* would demonstrate precision.

Many of the Woolf Report's recommendations have been implemented via the Civil Procedure Act 1997, which set out a framework by which rules of court could be made. The main provisions of this Act are set out in the table below.

Section	Comment
Section 1(1)	Established the *Civil Procedure Rules* to govern the practice and procedure for the Court of Appeal (Civil Division), the High Court and the county courts.
Section 1(3)	Makes it clear that the CPR exists 'with a view to securing that the civil justice system is *accessible, clear and efficient*'.
Section 2	Established the *Civil Procedure Rules Committee*, whose function is to make the CPR. The Committee must include persons 'with experience in and knowledge of' consumer affairs and lay advice as well as those with legal qualifications or holding particular judicial office.
Section 2 (7)	Imposes a duty on the Committee to make rules which are *'both simple and clearly expressed'*.
Section 6	Established the *Civil Justice Council*, whose primary functions are to continually review the civil justice system and consider how to make the system more accessible, fair and efficient, advise the Lord Chancellor and propose research. As with the CPR Committee, the Council must include laypersons as well as those 'able to represent the interests of particular kinds of litigants (for example, businesses or employees)'.

The Civil Procedure Rules 1998 (SI 1998, No. 3132) (as amended) came into force on 26 April 1999. Since then they have undergone 58 updates, and comprise 76 parts, together with a number of associated practice directions and eight pre-action protocols. The fifty-eighth update came into force on 6 April 2012 and introduced changes in a large number of areas including the implementation of the Terrorism Prevention and Investigation Measures Act 2011 and rules to facilitate the processing of work through the County Court Money Claims Centre.

Make your answer stand out

The latest version of the full text of the CPR can be found on the Ministry of Justice website at http://www.justice.gov.uk/guidance/courts-and-tribunals/courts/procedure-rules/civil/. The current text of each of the Rules we revise in the remainder of the chapter can be found here.

The overriding objective

Part 1 of the CPR emphasises their primary purpose as a new procedural code with the overriding objective of enabling the court to deal with cases 'justly'. In this instance, dealing with a case justly includes, so far as is practicable:

- ensuring that the parties are on an equal footing;
- saving expense;
- dealing with the case in ways which are proportionate to the amount of money involved, to the importance of the case, to the complexity of the issues, and to the financial position of each party;
- ensuring that it is dealt with expeditiously and fairly; and
- allotting to it an appropriate share of the court's resources, while taking into account the need to allot resources to other cases.

Courts must seek to further the objective of dealing with cases justly in exercising their powers or interpreting the rules themselves and by managing cases 'actively'.

Civil litigation

See the flowchart in Figure 7.1.

Starting proceedings

This is governed by *Part 7* of the CPR, *How to start proceedings – the claim form*.

The claim form

Civil proceedings are started when the court issues a claim form at the request of the claimant. The particulars of the claim (known as a 'statement of case') must be served either with the claim form or within 14 days of service of the claim form. The form and particulars must generally be served on (i.e. delivered to) the defendant within four months of issue (unless it is to be served outside the jurisdiction, where the time limit is extended to six months).

Figure 7.1

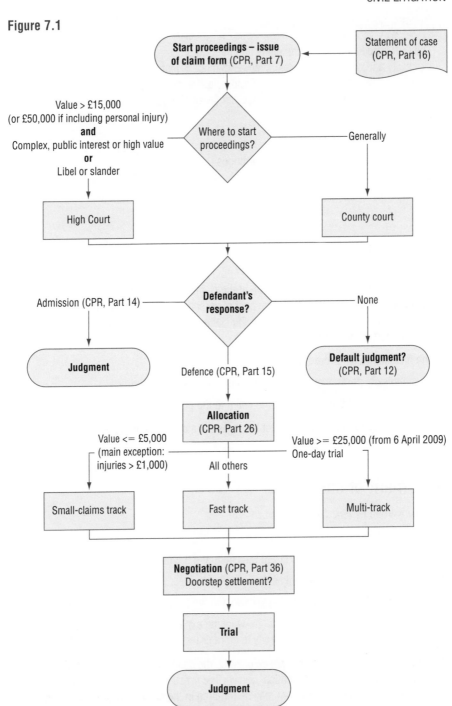

The CPR introduced new terminology into the civil process in an attempt to enable simplicity and clarity of expression. Although modern texts and articles tend to use the new terminology, it is important to appreciate some of the former terminology in case you encounter it in older cases or other areas of legal study. Some of the major changes are listed here:

- 'claimant' – formerly 'plaintiff';
- 'claim form' – formerly 'writ' or 'summons';
- 'statements of case' – formerly 'pleadings'.

Choice of court

Civil proceedings must generally be started in the county court. Proceedings may not be started in the High Court unless the value of the claim is more than £25,000 (or £50,000 for claims which include damages in respect of personal injuries). Even if this is so, claims should only be started in the High Court if the claimant believes that it ought to be dealt with by a High Court judge by reason of:

- the financial value of the claim; and/or
- its complexity (facts, legal issues, remedies or procedures); and/or
- the importance of the outcome of the claim to the public in general.

Claims involving libel or slander cannot be started in a county court unless the parties to the dispute have agreed so in writing.

Statement of case

This is governed by *Part 16* of the CPR.

The claim form must contain:

- a concise statement of the nature of the claim and the facts of the case;
- the remedy which the claimant seeks;
- the amount of money which he is claiming and the amount he expects to recover;
- a statement as to whether the amount which he expects to recover as general damages for pain, suffering and loss of amenity is more or less than (or equal to) £1,000.

The information in the claim form will be used by the courts in deciding how to allocate the case (see the section on 'Allocation' below). The practice direction accompanying Part 16 specifies further information that may be required in the claim form, depending on the nature of the claim. For instance, different additional information is required in the case of personal injury, fatal accident and hire-purchase claims.

 Make your answer stand out

The accompanying practice directions may also be found on the Ministry of Justice website at http://www.justice.gov.uk/civil/procrules_fin/menus/cpr_index.htm. These provide further clarification as to how the rules work in practice and provide a useful insight into their application.

Defendant's response

Within 14 days of service the defendant must:

- admit the claim (*Part 14*);
- defend the claim (*Part 15*); or
- file acknowledgment of service if he is unable to file a defence within the specified period or if he wishes to dispute the jurisdiction of the court (*Part 10*).

Default judgment

This is governed by *Part 12* of the CPR.

A default judgment is judgment without trial, where a defendant has failed to file an acknowledgment of service or a defence. The claimant should apply to the court and ask it to grant his claim. However, there are certain circumstances in which it is not possible to obtain a default judgment: most commonly in claims for delivery of goods subject to an agreement regulated by the Consumer Credit Act 1974 (that is, consumer credit and consumer hire agreements for amounts up to £25,000).

Allocation

This is governed by *Part 26* of the CPR.

Once the court has received the defendant's defence, procedural judges will allocate the case to one of three *tracks*:

- the small-claims track;
- the fast track; or
- the multi-track.

Each track provides a different level of case management. Remember that the overriding objective in Part 1 of the CPR requires the courts to take an active management role in civil cases.

7 CIVIL PROCEDURE

Before allocating a case to a particular track, the parties may request (or the court may consider of its own initiative) a **stay** while the parties try to settle the case by alternative dispute resolution (see section below) or other means.

> **KEY DEFINITION: Stay**
>
> A stay imposes a halt on proceedings, apart from taking any steps allowed by the Rules or the terms of the stay. Proceedings can be continued if a stay is lifted. A stay will generally be for one month, although the court does have discretion to order a stay for any period that it considers appropriate.

The allocation of the case will be determined by taking a number of factors into consideration, including:

- the financial value of the claim;
- the nature of the remedy sought;
- the likely complexity of the facts, law or evidence;
- the number of parties or likely parties;
- the value of any counterclaim;
- the amount of oral evidence which may be required;
- the importance of the claim to persons who are not parties to the proceedings;
- the views expressed by the parties; and
- the circumstances of the parties.

The scope of each track is as follows:

Track	Scope
Small-claims track	Any claim for personal injuries where: ■ the total value of the claim is not more than £5,000; and ■ the value of any claim for damages for personal injuries is not more than £1,000 Any claim which includes a claim by a residential tenant against a landlord where: ■ the tenant is seeking an order for the landlord to carry out repairs or other work to the premises; ■ the estimated cost of the work is not over £1,000; and ■ the value of any other claim for damages is not more than £1,000. Subject to the above, any claim which has a value of not more than £5,000.

Track	Scope
Fast track	Any claim which:
	■ falls outside the scope of the small-claims track;
	■ has a financial value of not more than £25,000 (for proceedings issued on or after 6 April 2009) or £15,000 (for proceedings issued before 6 April 2009);
	■ is likely to be tried in one day.
	Claims in the fast track also limit oral expert evidence at trial to two expert fields, with one expert per party in relation to each field.
Multi-track	Any claim which falls outside the small-claims track or the fast track. Therefore, the multi-track is generally used for higher value, more complex claims. Most commercial cases will fall within the multi-track.

The exact procedural steps that a case will follow depend on the track to which it is allocated. However, in each of the tracks, the court will provide standard directions relating to disclosure and inspection of documents relating to the case, exchange of statements from the witnesses that each side intends to call to give oral evidence and any reports from experts. The directions in multi-track cases are likely to be more complex and could involve *pre-trial reviews* or *case management conferences*.

 Make your answer stand out

For a more detailed description of the procedure that will be followed in each track, you should refer to the CPR as follows:

■ small-claims track – CPR, Part 27;
■ fast track – CPR, Part 28;
■ multi-track – CPR, Part 29.

Offers to settle and payments into court (Part 36 payments)

Generally speaking, both sides will wish to negotiate a settlement and avoid going to court. Not only do legal costs increase over time, but also claimants and defendants can find the process of trial stressful (particularly if a claimant has been injured) and the outcome of a trial is often far from certain. It can often be tempting for either side to 'cut their losses' and take a reasonable offer to settle out of court.

Part 36 of the CPR provides an incentive for parties to reach an out-of-court settlement. Under Part 36, the court will take into account any pre-action offers to settle when making an order for costs. In other words, the court will look less favourably upon a side that has refused a reasonable offer to settle when considering to what extent their costs should be paid by the other side.

This operates as follows:

- The defendant pays a sum of money (*the Part 36 payment*) into court as an offer of final settlement of the claimant's claim.

- The claimant has a set period (usually 21 days) in which to decide whether to accept the money paid into court or to pursue the case to trial.

- If the claimant refuses the Part 36 payment and, at trial, is awarded the same amount or less than the Part 36 payment, the claimant will normally have to pay his own costs *and those of the defendant from the latest date on which he could have accepted the payment.*

Therefore, a Part 36 payment is a significant tactical device which a defendant can use to try and reach an out-of-court settlement. The claimant has to judge whether to accept the payment or gamble on proceeding to trial with the risk of being awarded a lower sum *and* being liable for the costs of both sides from the time of the payment into court.

Part 36 also allows a claimant to make a *Part 36 offer*. If accepted by the defendant, the claimant will recover his costs up to the date of acceptance. If the matter proceeds to trial and the claimant is awarded more than this Part 36 offer, then the court can order the defendant to pay additional interest (of up to 10% above the Bank of England base rate) on the damages and costs awarded from the date upon which the defendant could have accepted the offer.

■ Stages of a civil trial

Stage	Comment
'Doorstep settlement'	It is often the case that the parties will agree a settlement at the very last minute, literally at the door to the courtroom.
Claimant's case – opening speech	There may be an opening speech on behalf of the claimant setting out the circumstances of the claim and any pertinent issues. However, opening speeches are less important in a civil trial since the judge will already be aware of all the documentary evidence surrounding the case and there will be no requirement to set the scene for a jury (although defamation trials in the High Court will have a jury present).

Stage	Comment
Claimant's case	Remember that witness statements have already been exchanged by this stage. Therefore, the statements stand as the evidence-in-chief. The claimant and any other witnesses will swear in turn that the statement is theirs and that they will stand by its contents. The claimant and any witnesses are then cross-examined in turn on behalf of the defendant (leading questions are allowed). Counsel for the claimant is then allowed (if so desired) to re-examine the witness (but only on matters arising from the cross-examination).
Defendant's case	Counsel for the defendant may make an opening speech in the same way as counsel for the claimant. He will call defence witnesses who will be examined-in-chief, cross-examined by the counsel for the claimant and re-examined by the defence.
Closing speeches	Counsel for the defendant and claimant will summarise the main points of their cases, and outline their view on the appropriate level of damages that should be awarded.
Judgment	The judge will deliver his judgment – either immediately, after an adjournment or, for complex cases, adjourned until a later date. Unlike criminal trials, judges give reasons for their decision. He will then make an award for damages and costs. Note that until the end of the trial the judge does *not* know whether there has been a Part 36 offer or a Part 36 payment. This information is kept from him in order to prevent it influencing his decision.
Appeal	The appeals system is covered in the following section.

■ The civil appeals system

The appeal system in civil cases was reformed by Part 52 of the Civil Procedure Rules 1998 and the accompanying Practice Direction. This came into force in May 2000. Certain aspects of procedure can also be found in the Access to Justice Act 1999 and its associated statutory instrument, the Access to Justice Act 1999 (Destination of Appeals) Order 2000.

Before explaining the various routes of appeal, you should consider the general principle that the route that a particular civil case will take on appeal will depend upon:

■ the seniority of the judge who made the original decision (district judge, circuit judge or High Court judge);

■ the court in which he sat when making that decision (county court or High Court).

> **📖 REVISION NOTE**
>
> You may wish to take a look at Chapter 5 and refresh your memory on judges and Chapter 3 on the jurisdictions and personnel of the civil courts at this stage. It will also be useful to make sure you understand the different tracks through the civil courts – specifically the small-claims track, the fast track and the multi-track. The track in which a case is heard may have a bearing on the route it takes on appeal so it is important that you are familiar both with the terms and their meaning.

The roles of each level of judge in the civil courts can be illustrated by way of a table as follows:

	County Court	**High Court**
District judge	Most pre-trial matters Cases involving claims up to £15,000 in value	Most pre-trial matters
Circuit judge	Cases involving claims in excess of £15,000 in value	
High Court judge		Civil trials

Civil routes of appeal

There are several routes which a civil case might take on appeal. This will depend on:

- the court in which the claimant began proceedings (that is, the county court or the High Court); and
- the level of judge who made the decision which is being appealed.

An overview of the routes is shown in Figure 7.2.

Appeals from the magistrates' court

- Appeals from the magistrates' court in family proceedings involving matters of fact or matters of law can be made to the Divisional Court of the Family Division of the High Court (s. 61, Senior Courts Act 1981).
- Appeals from the magistrates' court in licensing (and other civil) matters can be made to the Crown Court (s. 45, Senior Courts Act 1981).

Figure 7.2

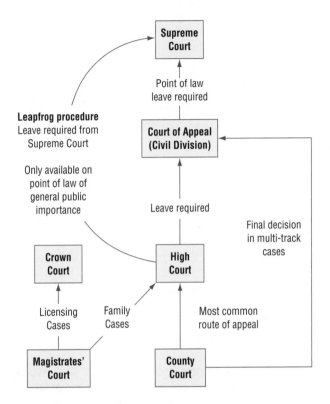

□ REVISION NOTE

The Senior Courts Act 1981 was formerly known as the Supreme Court Act 1981. Its title was changed on 1 October 2009 by the Constitutional Reform Act 2005.

Appeals from the county court

■ Appeals against the decision of a district judge made in the county court can be made to a circuit judge *and will usually be held within the county court* (Access to Justice Act 1999 (Destination of Appeals) Order 2000).

■ Appeals against a decision of a circuit judge made in the county court can be made to a High Court judge *and will usually be held within the High Court* (Access to Justice Act 1999 (Destination of Appeals) Order 2000).

■ Appeals against the decision of a district judge made in the High Court can be made to a High Court judge *and will usually be held within the High Court* (Access to Justice Act 1999 (Destination of Appeals) Order 2000).

- Appeals against a *final* decision of a district judge or circuit judge made in a case *allocated to the multi-track* in the county court can be made directly to the Court of Appeal (Civil Division).

Appeals from the High Court

- Appeals against the decision of a High Court judge can generally be made to the Court of Appeal (Civil Division).

The 'leapfrog' procedure

In certain circumstances an appeal may be made directly from the High Court to the Supreme Court, effectively 'leapfrogging' the Court of Appeal (Civil Division) (Part II, ss. 12, 13, 15, Administration of Justice Act 1969).

The leapfrog procedure is only available if:

- the trial judge grants a certificate. This will only be done with the consent of all parties and the case involves a point of general public interest – such points will be concerned with either matters of statutory interpretation (see Chapter 1) or the operation of a precedent set by an earlier case in either the Court of Appeal (Civil Division) or the Supreme Court (House of Lords); and
- the Supreme Court grants leave to appeal.

The leapfrog procedure provides a shortcut for cases that would, in all probability, ultimately have ended up being considered in the Supreme Court via the Court of Appeal (Civil Division). It therefore offers savings in terms of both time and expense; however, despite this, it is still used relatively infrequently. A relatively recent example can be found in *R (on the application of Alconbury Developments Ltd) v. Secretary of State for Environment, Transport and the Regions* [2003] 2 AC 295, HL. It could be argued that this may be because High Court judges fail to recognise the potential importance of particular cases when they are before them and thus do not grant the appropriate certificates to initiate the leapfrog procedure. The importance of a particular case is often only uncovered by the Court of Appeal (Civil Division), by which time it is too late for the leapfrog procedure to be used.

Appeals from the Court of Appeal (Civil Division)

Appeals against the decision of the Court of Appeal (Civil Division) can be made directly to the Supreme Court. These appeals will generally concern a point of law. Leave to appeal must be granted by the Court of Appeal (Civil Division) or the Supreme Court. Unusually, there is no statutory requirement that the appeal concerns a matter of general public importance. In practice, leave to appeal is generally only granted to those cases that do raise such issues (*Practice Direction (HL: Petition for Leave to Appeal)* [1988] 1 WLR 939, HL).

Second appeals

Following a civil appeal against the decision of a district judge or circuit judge within the county courts or the decision of a district judge within the High Court, there is generally *no right* to a second appeal. This was confirmed by the judgments of the Court of Appeal (Civil Division) in *Tanfern Ltd* v. *Cameron-MacDonald* [2000] 1 WLR 1311, CA and *Clark* v. *Perks* [2001] 1 WLR 17, CA.

Second appeals, where granted, are heard by the Court of Appeal (Civil Division). However, under s. 55 of the Access to Justice Act 1999, permission for a second appeal must be granted by the Court of Appeal (Civil Division) and will not be granted unless:

- the appeal would raise an important point of principle or practice; or
- there is some other compelling reason for the Court of Appeal to hear the appeal.

Powers of appeal courts in civil matters

Every appeal court effectively has the same set of powers. In effect, the appeal court has all the powers of the lower court, meaning that it may, for example:

- affirm, set aside or vary any order or judgment made or given by the lower court;
- refer any claim or issue for determination by the lower court;
- order a new trial or hearing.

The appeal court will not normally allow the hearing of oral evidence or the presentation of any documentary evidence that was not put before the lower court.

■ Putting it all together

Answer guidelines

See the sample question at the start of the chapter. A diagram illustrating how to structure your answer is available on the companion website.

Approaching the question

This problem question involves a detailed knowledge of the civil process and the allocation of claims to a particular track through the civil courts. Look back at Figure 7.1 for an overview.

▶

Important points to include

- Include each stage in the likely sequence of events and consider the 'what if?' scenarios carefully. For instance, the defendant might choose not, or forget, to respond to the claim, in which case you can discuss default judgments under CPR Part 12. If you had assumed (as many students would) that the defendant would enter a defence then you could be missing out part of the answer.

- The final parts of the question are designed to test your knowledge of the allocation of civil cases to the appropriate track. The real trick here is in part (b). The unwary student would look at the total value of claim at £3,400 and allocate it to the small-claims track. However, the value of the personal injury claim is over £1,000, so regardless of the total value of the claim, it cannot fall within the small-claims track.

 Make your answer stand out

- Consider all potential steps in the likely sequence of events and be as detailed as possible in your answer.
- Refer to authority (typically relevant parts of the CPR).
- Discuss where Sue needs to bring a claim (in the county court) and why she would not be able to bring a claim in the High Court. This demonstrates a much greater attention to detail and conveys the fact that you understand the rules on where claims are commenced and why that is.
- There are a number of possible events shown in Figure 7.1. Be as thorough as you can.

READ TO IMPRESS

Abel, R. (1973) 'The comparative study of dispute institutions in society', 8 *Law and Society Rev* 217.

Flemming, J. (2000) 'Judge airs concerns over Woolf reforms', *Law Society Gazette* 10 February.

Harrison, R. (1999) 'Why have two types of civil court?', 149 *New Law Journal* 65.

Pedley, F.H. (1994) 'The small claims process', 144 *New Law Journal* 1217.

---

www.pearsoned.co.uk/lawexpress

 Go online to access more revision support including quizzes to test your knowledge, sample questions with answer guidelines, podcasts you can download, and more!

Tribunals and alternative dispute resolution

8

Revision checklist

Essential points you should know:

- [ ] The rationale behind the tribunals system
- [ ] The advantages and disadvantages of tribunals
- [ ] The operation of the First-tier Tribunal and the Upper Tribunal
- [ ] The different means of alternative dispute resolution: arbitration, mediation and conciliation

■ Topic map

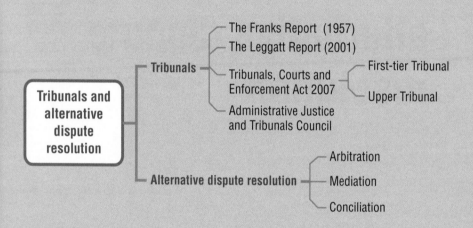

■ Introduction

Parties in dispute do not have to pursue an action through the courts

As well as the court system which you revised in Chapter 3, there are various alternative ways in which disputes can be resolved. This chapter begins by looking at the tribunal system which deals with a very broad range of cases in particular areas of law. Although there has been a system of tribunals in place for some time, it has recently been overhauled and reorganised via the Tribunals, Courts and Enforcement Act 2007. The chapter then goes on to consider the three main forms of Alternative Dispute Resolution (ADR): arbitration, mediation and conciliation.

ASSESSMENT ADVICE

The nature of the tribunals and ADR are such that they are much more likely to be assessed by an essay question than in a problem scenario. The common theme between them is that they have both undergone recent scrutiny by way of official report: the tribunals system has been overhauled in response to the recommendations of the Leggatt Report, and ADR has been mentioned (in the broader context of civil litigation in general) in the Jackson Report. It is important that you understand the problems with the systems which led to the commissioning of these reports, as well as the recommendations that the reports made and the consequences of implementing those recommendations. It is not enough to be able to describe the current mechanisms for tribunals or ADR: you need to be able to engage in a critical debate about their strengths and weaknesses and show an awareness and understanding of the reforms that are taking place.

■ Sample question

Could you answer this question? Below is a typical essay question that could arise on this topic. Guidelines on answering the question are included at the end of this chapter, whilst a further sample question and guidance on tackling it can be found on the companion website.

◼ Tribunals

It is usual to think of legal disputes being settled in the courts. However, there are other mechanisms for resolution, including tribunals. These are an alternative to using the 'traditional' courts and their use is, in fact, mandatory in certain types of dispute.

Many disputes are dealt with in the network of tribunals that evolved throughout the twentieth century. Each tribunal dealt with a particular area of specialism such as employment, rent, immigration and mental health.

Tribunals were seen as a more effective way of dealing with specialist disputes, as they had particular expertise to deal with the intricacies of the law and a better understanding of the types of disputes that would come before them. They adopted less formal procedures to hear and decide cases more quickly: this, in turn, helped to minimise costs. The lack of formality also meant that, in theory at least, there would be less need for legal representation.

❗ Don't be tempted to . . .

The term 'tribunal' does not necessarily mean something different to a court. For instance, some tribunals have been considered to be courts for the purposes of contempt, and the Employment Appeal Tribunal is also a superior court of record. So, although, any type of court can be called a tribunal (especially in Europe – see Chapter 2) it is usually used to refer to bodies with specialist jurisdiction and which often contains both qualified and lay (non-lawyer) members.

The Franks Report

The function of tribunals was first reviewed in depth by the Franks Committee (1957). It described them as:

> [Not] ordinary courts, but neither . . . appendages of Government Departments . . . Tribunals should properly be regarded as machinery provided by Parliament for adjudication rather than as part of the machinery of administration.

The Franks Report made a number of recommendations for the reform of the tribunal system that would ensure that it had three key characteristics:

- fairness
- openness
- impartiality.

It also listed the strengths of the tribunal system as cheapness, accessibility, freedom from technicality, expedition (being able to deal with cases relatively quickly; at least compared to the court system) and expert knowledge of their own area of jurisdiction.

Its recommendations were implemented by the Tribunals and Inquiries Act 1958. Later changes were also introduced by the Tribunals and Inquiries Act 1992.

The Leggatt Report (2001)

The number of tribunals continued to proliferate as new tribunals were introduced by legislation to deal with particular disputes. For example, the Mental Health Act 1983 created the Mental Health Review Tribunal, with responsibility for hearing applications from people who had been detained under the Act against their wishes.

Each tribunal operated under the rules stipulated by the particular piece of legislation that created it. For example, there were no uniform rules concerning the availability of appeals against tribunal decisions or the procedures by which an appeal could be brought.

These concerns of lack of consistency were addressed by Sir Andrew Leggatt, who headed a review of the tribunal system. The aim of its report *Tribunals for Users: One System, One Service* (2001) (often referred to simply as 'the Leggatt Report') was to recommend a system that was 'coherent, professional, cost effective and user-friendly' and which would also be compatible with the Convention right to a fair trial under Article 6 ECHR.

Leggatt recommended that the tribunal system should be unified into a single administrative body that would deal with around 300,000 cases each year.

Tribunals, Courts and Enforcement Act 2007

The recommendations of the Leggatt Report were enacted by the Tribunals, Courts and Enforcement Act 2007. Within the new structure, the functions of the majority of pre-existing tribunals were transferred to the new First-tier Tribunal created by s. 3 of the Act.

First-tier Tribunal

This First-tier Tribunal is organised into various Chambers, each with its own area of specialism.

General Regulatory Chamber	Alternative business structures
	Charity
	Claims management services
	Consumer credit
	Environment
	Estate agents
	Gambling appeals
	Immigration services
	Information rights
	Local Government standards in England
	Transport
Social Entitlement Chamber	Asylum support
	Criminal injuries compensation
	Social security and child support
Health, Education and Social Care Chamber	Care standards
	Mental health
	Special educational needs and disability
	Primary health lists
War Pensions and Armed Forces Compensation Chamber	War pensions and armed forces compensation
Tax Chamber	Tax
	MP expenses
Immigration and Asylum Chamber	Immigration
	Asylum

It is envisaged that further tribunals will be added to the new structure as part of a phased implementation programme.

Upper Tribunal

Section 11 of the Act created an Upper Tribunal, which provides the normal route of appeal from decisions made by the First-tier Tribunal on a point of law. However, some decisions (such as decisions relating to asylum support and criminal injuries compensation) do not carry a right to appeal and can therefore only be challenged via judicial review. Some cases commence directly in the Upper Tribunal.

The Upper Tribunal is divided into four Chambers:

- Administrative Appeals Chamber
- Tax and Chancery Chamber
- Immigration and Asylum Chamber
- Lands Chamber

Section 13 of the Act provides that a route of appeal will lie from decisions of the Chambers of the Upper Tribunal to the Civil Division of the Court of Appeal on a point of law. See Figure 8.1 for an overview of the general structure.

Figure 8.1

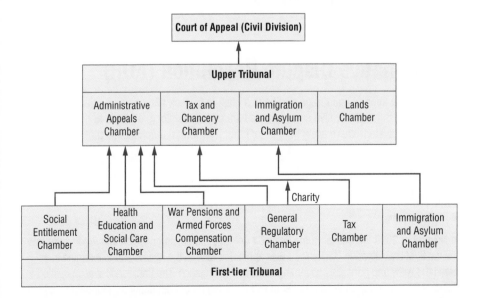

Make your answer stand out

Full details on the work of each of chambers within the First-tier and Upper Tribunals can be found on the HM Courts & Tribunals Service website at http://www.justice .gov.uk/guidance/courts-and-tribunals/tribunals/index.htm. This site contains a wealth of further detail that could particularly enhance your answer and demonstrate your depth of knowledge on the detailed operation of the tribunals system.

Administrative Justice and Tribunals Council

Section 44 of the Tribunals, Courts and Enforcement Act 2007 creates the Administrative Justice and Tribunals Council. This is a public body with responsibility for supervising and regulating the administrative justice system. In relation to the new tribunal system, the Council must review and report on the operation of the tribunals under its supervision and scrutinise legislation relating to tribunals.

 Make your answer stand out

There is a comprehensive discussion of the impact of the Tribunals, Courts and Enforcement Act 2007 by the Senior President of Tribunals, Sir Robert Carnwath (2009) which would make excellent reading in preparation for an essay on the topic.

■ Alternative Dispute Resolution (ADR)

The courts are keen to encourage parties to a dispute to seek alternative means of resolution without using the ordinary civil court system wherever possible. In addition to the courts and tribunals system, there are a number of other less formal mechanisms that may be employed:

- arbitration
- mediation
- conciliation.

In November 2008 the Master of the Rolls, Sir Anthony Clarke, commissioned a report to review the costs of civil litigation. Jackson LJ was appointed to lead the review and to examine in detail the rules and principles governing costs in civil litigation. The final report was published in January 2010 and contained a number of wide-ranging recommendations. Amongst these is the recommendation that a 'serious campaign' should be undertaken to ensure that both lawyers and judges fully understand how all forms of alternative dispute resolution work and the benefits it can bring. Jackson suggests that a 'handbook for ADR' should be prepared for use by clients and as a training guide for lawyers and the judiciary, along with a simple and clear brochure to educate the public and small businesses about ADR. Despite the benefits of ADR benefits, Jackson does not recommend that parties should be compelled to mediate.

Arbitration

Arbitration is the longest established form of ADR; there has been some form of Arbitration Act since 1889. In arbitration, the disputing parties agree to have the case heard by a neutral third party for resolution, rather than pursuing it in the ordinary civil courts. In the case of contractual disputes, the contract will often state an agreed arbitration procedure. If not, the parties can still agree to go to arbitration once the dispute has arisen.

The arbitration procedure is governed by the Arbitration Act 1996 which sets out the principles of arbitration as follows:

- the object of arbitration is to obtain the fair resolution of disputes by an impartial tribunal without necessary delay or expense;
- the parties should be free to agree how their disputes are resolved, subject only to such safeguards as are necessary in the public interest;
- the court should not generally intervene unless the arbitration process fails to reach a just settlement or legal assistance is required.

Arbitration awards are enforceable through the civil courts.

Lord Hoffman identified the nature of arbitration in *Premium Nafta Products Ltd* v. *Fili Shipping Co Ltd* [2007] UKHL 40:

> Arbitration is consensual. It depends on the intention of the parties as expressed in their agreement. Only the agreement can tell you what kind of disputes they intended to submit to arbitration. But the meaning which the parties intended to express by the words which they used will be affected by the commercial background and the readers' understanding of the purpose for which the agreement was made.

Some advantages of arbitration

Advantage	Comment
Informality	Arbitration proceedings are less formal than those in the civil courts
Speed	Arbitration generally results in a settlement far more quickly than an action in the civil courts ▶

Advantage	Comment
Cost	Although the use of arbitration often carries a cost (particularly where specialist arbitrators are used), it is still usually cheaper than using the courts
Expertise	Arbitrators are usually specialists in the field under dispute; they, therefore, can use their expert knowledge in reaching a conclusion
Privacy	Since arbitration hearings are usually conducted in private, commercial organisations, in particular, can be assured that there is no risk of adverse publicity

Procedure

The arbitrator resolves the dispute and makes an award, seeking legal advice if necessary. If an important point of law arises during the arbitration, the arbitrator can 'state a case' – that is, make reference to the court for its opinion on the law which is then applied to the facts of the case.

The decision of the arbitrator is final and binding. However, the court can set aside an award (in whole or in part) if there has been a 'serious irregularity' in procedure (Arbitration Act 1996, s. 68). This includes:

- failure by the tribunal to comply with the general duty of the tribunal
- the tribunal exceeding its powers
- failure by the tribunal to conduct the proceedings in accordance with the procedure agreed by the parties
- failure by the tribunal to deal with all the issues that were put to it
- any arbitral or other institution or person vested by the parties with powers in relation to the proceedings or the award exceeding its powers
- uncertainty or ambiguity as to the effect of the award
- the award being obtained by fraud or the award or the way in which it was procured being contrary to public policy
- failure to comply with the requirements as to the form of the award
- any irregularity in the conduct of the proceedings or in the award which is admitted by the tribunal or by any arbitral or other institution or person vested by the parties with powers in relation to the proceedings or the award.

Mediation

Mediation is much more informal than the other forms of ADR. In mediation, a third party acts as a 'go between' through which the parties attempt to negotiate a resolution to the problem. Mediation may take place either in the presence of the parties, or without them having to meet. The most common mediation scheme is that relating to divorcing couples. The Family Law Act 1996 increased the emphasis on couples to attempt to reach a mediated settlement to avoid having one imposed upon them by the courts. However, in a pilot study, only 10% of couples were willing to enter 'preliminary information meetings' (which the Family Law Act intended to make compulsory); of these only 7% opted for mediation, and the mediation proposals in the Act were abandoned in January 2001. It is also interesting to note that almost 40% of couples attending the meetings were *more convinced* of the need to seek professional legal help to protect their rights.

Conciliation

Conciliation is a form of ADR that lies between mediation and arbitration. In conciliation, the third party may suggest a non-binding settlement which the parties may agree (unlike mediation where the parties largely have to devise their own solution). Conciliation differs from arbitration in that it has no formal legal standing, there is no provision for witnesses or evidence and there is no award of compensation or damages.

One of the most well-known organisations which offers mediation and conciliation in relation to employment disputes is the Advisory Conciliation and Arbitration Service (more commonly referred to as Acas) which was established in 1975, although a voluntary conciliation and arbitration service was first launched by the government in 1896. It has a statutory function under the Employment Rights (Dispute Resolution) Act 1998 to try to resolve employment disputes before a full tribunal hearing and at present 75% are settled or withdrawn at the Acas stage.

 Make your answer stand out

For an excellent overview of the way in which Acas gets involved in dispute resolution in the field of employment visit: http://www.acas.org.uk/index.aspx?articleid=2006 (arbitration) and http://www.acas.org.uk/index.aspx?articleid=1697 (conciliation).

■ Putting it all together

Answer guidelines

See the sample question at the start of the chapter.

Approaching the question

This question requires you to consider the extent to which the Tribunals, Courts and Enforcement Act 2007 has improved the 'situation' referred to in the quotation from the Leggatt Report. This means that you need to evaluate the reforms that have been introduced in response to that report by the Act against the criticisms raised by the quotation: specifically, haphazard growth, varied practice and lack of coherence.

Important points to include

One possible structure for this essay could be:

- An introduction which analyses the quotation and sets out the structure that is to follow: remember that you need not only to describe what the current tribunals system looks like following implementation of the 2007 Act, but also how it addresses the criticisms levelled at the previous system.

- Explain how the tribunals system evolved following the Franks Report: as particular disputes arose, legislation was introduced to deal with each in turn (haphazard).

- Each tribunal had its own operating rules that were set by its enabling legislation (varied practice).

- This was particularly problematic in relation to the appeals processes which had no uniform procedure for bringing an appeal or single set of rules that determined availability (almost no coherence).

- Explain how this led to the Leggatt Report and its aims of coherence, professionalism, cost-effectiveness and user-friendliness.

- Move on to discuss the recommendation of the Report and how this was implemented via the two-tier system set out in the 2007 Act with various Chambers, all of which have clearly defined processes and procedures as well as uniform routes of appeal as far as the Court of Appeal (Civil Division).

- Consider whether the new system is less haphazard, consistent in practice and coherent.

- Conclude by setting out your view on whether the Leggatt recommendations achieved the aims of the report or whether you consider there still to be flaws within the current system.

Make your answer stand out

The difference between a good answer and an outstanding answer to an essay question such as this one will often depend on the relative balance of critical evaluation and analysis versus description. While you might be able to list the various Chambers of the new two-tier Tribunal System, this is only part of the task. You should make sure that you are able not only to say what the current system is, but also how it was before, why that was problematic and whether the reforms have actually achieved their purpose. This will mean that you need to be familiar with the material as well as ensuring that you tightly refer back to the quotation that is provided in the question and not simply producing a description of the Tribunals system in the abstract. In addition, you could also draw reference to the article by Sir Robert Carnwath to add further authority to your answer, particularly if you have a useful and relevant quote that you can deploy – this will show clear evidence of further reading which is always welcomed.

READ TO IMPRESS

Carnwarth, R. (2009) 'Tribunal Justice: A New Start' *Public Law* 48.

Department of Constitutional Affairs (2004) *Transforming Public Services: Complaints, Redress and Tribunals* (Cm 6243), London: HMSO.

Leggatt, A. (2001) *Tribunals for Users: One System, One Service,* London: HMSO.

Ministry of Justice (2007) *Transforming Tribunals, Implementing Part 1 of the Tribunals, Courts and Enforcement Act 2007* CP 30/07, London: HMSO.

www.pearsoned.co.uk/lawexpress

 Go online to access more revision support including quizzes to test your knowledge, sample questions with answer guidelines, podcasts you can download, and more!

Access to justice

9

■ Topic map

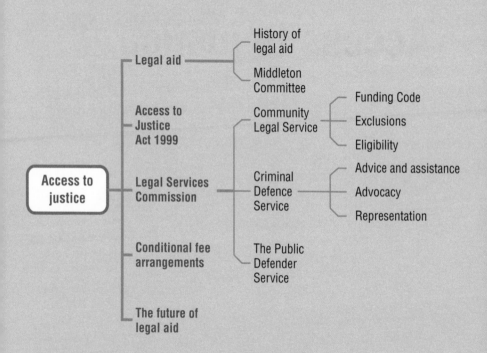

■ Introduction

Access to legal advice is a fundamental right under Article 6 of the European Convention on Human Rights

If a person cannot get access to legal advice when needed then there would clearly be a flaw in the system: otherwise people would be unsure (or even unaware) of their legal rights and obligations and could not take advantage of the system of courts and tribunals that exist to promote justice for all.

The cost of litigation can be very high: costs in personal injury cases often exceed £20,000 and can easily be double this in medical negligence cases. It is not just the cost of professional legal advice that needs to be met: court fees and other expenses contribute to substantial overall costs. It is for this reason that enabling access to justice is a challenge for the state.

ASSESSMENT ADVICE

It is almost certain that the topic of access to justice would be examined by means of an essay question. The whole topic is characterised by the perennial difficulty of balancing the right to justice (and thus to legal advice) against the cost to the state of doing so. As such the whole legal aid structure has undergone several reforms. It is important that you bear in mind the social, political and financial context in which the various sets of reform have been proposed and implemented as well as the actual detail of the reforms themselves and the way in which the system currently operates. As this is an area that looks as if it is about to be comprehensively reviewed and reformed during the lifetime of this particular edition, it is important that you are aware of current developments and able to draw reference to them where relevant in your answers. The ability to show knowledge and understanding of current debate is important.

■ Sample question

Could you answer this question? Below is a typical essay question that could arise on this topic. Guidelines on answering the question are included at the end of this chapter, whilst a further sample question and guidance on tackling it can be found on the companion website.

Legal aid

Legal aid has been the main mechanism by which individuals have been able to secure affordable access to professional legal assistance.

History of legal aid

Legal aid was introduced as part of the development of the welfare state after the Second World War. Before then, legal advice was only available if individual lawyers would generously accept a case for a reduced, or no, fee.

The system evolved through a series of statutes:

Legal Aid and Advice Act 1949	Created the civil legal aid scheme
Legal Advice and Assistance Act 1972; Legal Aid Acts 1960, 1964, 1974, 1979	Expanded the system of civil legal aid
Criminal Justice Act 1967	Created the criminal legal aid scheme
Legal Aid Act 1988	Established a unified scheme covering both civil and criminal cases

Middleton Committee Report

In 1997 the Middleton Committee reported to the Lord Chancellor following its review of civil justice and legal aid. It raised a number of concerns with the legal aid scheme as it had evolved, but particularly:

- That the costs of legal aid were increasing rapidly, but the number of people assisted were decreasing
- The scheme did not target resources on priority areas

- The rules for eligibility (means testing) meant that access to justice was restricted to the very poor and those rich enough to pay for themselves (leaving out a large middle section of the population).

The government responded to the Middleton Report by publishing its *Modernising Justice* White Paper in 1998. This contained a whole package of reforms, but included a strategy to reduce the cost of justice for all, and thus make it more accessible and reduce the overall legal aid expenditure. The proposals were brought into being by the Access to Justice Act 1999.

Legal Services Commission

The Access to Justice Act 1999 established the Legal Services Commission (LSC) which is required to establish, maintain and develop two services:

- Community Legal Service (CLS)
- Criminal Defence Service (CDS)

The LSC is a non-departmental public body sponsored by the Ministry of Justice.

Publicly funded services can only be provided by those who are under contract to the LSC. These contracts restrict both the types of cases that individual providers may take on and the number of cases. This 'preferred supplier' scheme is designed to assist in controlling budgets and quality of service.

The LSC has particular targets against which it measures its effectiveness. For example, its recent targets included initatives to:

- Increase the number of refuges with access to family/social welfare law advice for domestic abuse victims by 10%
- Reduce the number of unnecessary adjournments at first-tier mental health tribunals by 30%
- Improve the efficiency of police station advice and assistance by nationally reducing the percentage of unanswered calls from CDS Direct by 10%.

Community Legal Service

The CLS has a statutory purpose to promote the availability of a range of services and to secure access to those services so as to effectively meet individual needs. These services comprise:

- the provision of general information about the law and legal system and the availability of legal services,
- the provision of help by the giving of advice as to how the law applies in particular circumstances,

- the provision of help in preventing, or settling or otherwise resolving, disputes about legal rights and duties,

- the provision of help in enforcing decisions by which such disputes are resolved, and

- the provision of help in relation to legal proceedings not relating to disputes.

Funding Code

The Funding Code is issued under section 8 of the 1999 Act and sets out the six types of service that may be funded by suppliers contracted to the LSC:

- Legal Help (provision of legal advice).

- Help at Court (help and advocacy for a particular hearing, but not so far as to be formal representation).

- Family Help – this can be either Family Help (Lower) or Family Help (Higher).

- Legal Representation – this can be either Investigative Help or Full Representation.

- Family Mediation.

- Such other services as are authorised by specific orders or directions from the Lord Chancellor.

Exclusions

As well as setting out the types of help that is available within the Funding Code, Schedule 2 to the 1999 Act lists those services for which help (over and above provision of general information about the law, the legal system and the availability of legal services) is **not** available:

- allegations of personal injury or death, other than allegations relating to clinical negligence;

- allegations of negligently caused damage to property;

- conveyancing;

- boundary disputes;

- the making of wills;

- matters of trust law;

- the creation of lasting powers of attorney under the Mental Capacity Act 2005;

- the making of advance decisions under that Act;

- defamation or malicious falsehood;

- matters of company or partnership law;

- attending an interview on a claim for asylum.

Eligibility

Individuals must satisfy both a merits test and a means test in order to obtain services via the CLS. Those with low income and little by way of financial resources are entitled to full CLS assistance, while some who are better-off may be required to contribute towards the services.

Criminal Defence Service

The Criminal Defence Service was also set up by the Access to Justice Act 1999. It is run by the LSC but is quite separate from the CLS. Like the CLS, it has contracted providers, but for criminal defence services.

It aims to ensure that people under police investigation or facing criminal charges can get legal advice and representation. Criminal legal aid offers:

- advice and assistance from a solicitor on criminal matters
- free legal advice from a solicitor at the police station during questioning
- the cost of a solicitor preparing a case and initial representation for certain proceedings at magistrates' or Crown Court
- full legal representation for defence in criminal cases at all court levels
- a duty solicitor to provide free legal advice and representation at magistrates' court.

There are three basic levels of service that can be provided:

- advice and assistance
- advocacy
- representation.

Advice and assistance

Probably the most important function of the CDS is the duty solicitor scheme. Police station duty solicitors consult with persons who have been is arrested on suspicion of a criminal offence, either in person or on the telephone whilst in police custody. Court duty solicitors consult with those that have already been charged with an offence and represent them on their first appearance at the magistrates' court if they do not have their own solicitor. These schemes are available free of charge and are not means tested.

Advocacy assistance

Duty solicitors may provide advocacy assistance in connection with bail and any CDS solicitor may provide advocacy assistance in relation to anti-social behaviour orders (ASBOs) or proceedings involving non-payment of fines.

Representation

Representation is subject to a test of merit and is granted by application to the magistrates' court. It is not means tested but costs can be recovered at the conclusion of a case by a recovery of defence costs order issued by the Crown Court.

The Criminal Defence Service Act 2006 introduced means testing in magistrates' courts and requires defendants who are convicted to repay their defence costs if they can afford to do so. Means testing was introduced in certain Crown Courts in 2010.

The Public Defender Service

The Public Defender Service (PDS) allows the CDS to provide criminal help through its own employed solicitors, accredited representatives and administrators. There are four PDS offices in Cheltenham, Darlington, Pontypridd and Swansea and it aims to provide services in areas that are less well supported by privately contracted providers.

 Make your answer stand out

Bridges *et al.* (2007) provide a useful evaluation of the Public Defender Service which gives a great deal of information about its operation and effectiveness.

■ Conditional fee arrangements

The Conditional Fee Agreements Regulations 2000 (SI 2000/692) established the 'no win, no fee' arrangements for pursuing civil law claims. This allows lawyers to offer conditional fee agreements in all civil matters, with the exception of family law cases. These have replaced legal aid in most types of litigation.

They work by allowing that the client's fees and expenses are only payable in certain circumstances. If the claim is successful, then the claimant will have to pay their solicitors' fees: these will be much higher than if the case had been lost. The success fee is an extra amount that is paid to the solicitor if the claim is successful. Success fees in 'no win, no fee' cases are often quite high, and can be as much as double the amount charged in other similar cases. This may not all be recoverable from the other party and any shortfall is paid from the damages awarded. Barristers' fees are usually not included in conditional fee agreements. Similarly other expenses such as experts' fees, accident report fees, official searches, court fees, and travelling expenses may not be included in the agreement and would have to be borne by the claimant.

The Ministry of Justice revealed plans to reform the no-win, no-fee system in March 2011 claiming it has enabled lawyers to profit massively by charging inflated fees that can be claimed back from the losing side.

📖 REVISION NOTE

It is likely that the regulation of conditional fee arrangements will change. Check to see if there have been any updates in this area.

■ The future of legal aid

In November 2010, the government published a Green Paper on legal aid which outlined proposals:

. . . to encourage people, rather than going to court too readily at the taxpayer's expense, to seek alternative methods of dispute resolution, reserving the courts as a last resort for legal issues where there is a public interest in providing access to public funding.

 Make your answer stand out

The Government's Green Paper encapsulates the problems well and would be good material with which to familiarise yourself in preparation for an essay question on the reform of the system.

The strategy, then, seems to keep people outside the court system (and thus keeping down costs) as much as possible.

📖 REVISION NOTE

This could combine with a discussion of alternative dispute resolution mechanisms. Refresh your memory on these in Chapter 8.

There are major changes proposed to civil legal aid, again designed to cut costs. The Legal Aid, Sentencing and Punishment of Offenders Bill is expected to receive Royal Assent in 2012. In particular it:

- reverses the position under the Access to Justice Act 1999, whereby civil legal aid is available for any matter not specifically excluded. The Bill takes some types of case out of scope for legal aid funding and provides that cases would not be eligible for funding unless of a type specified in the Bill
- abolishes the Legal Services Commission
- makes various provisions in respect of civil litigation funding and costs.

The Bill removes legal aid from cases concerning employment, housing (except in cases involving homelessness or risk to health and safety), debt (except in cases relating to certain proceedings where the home is at risk), and welfare benefits.

> 📖 **REVISION NOTE**
>
> Make sure that you stay in touch with the current position on the passage of the Bill and its impact by following its progress on the Parliament website: http://services. parliament.uk/bills/2010-11/legalaidsentencingandpunishmentofoffenders.html.

■ Putting it all together

Answer guidelines

See the sample question at the start of the chapter.

Approaching the question

This question contains a quotation which you are required to evaluate critically. As with any question like this, you should break the quotation down into its constituent parts and make sure that you plan your essay to cover each of them. This will ensure that you stay focused and relevant to the particular essay that has been set, rather than falling into the common trap of 'writing all you know about access to justice'. The key parts of the quotation that you need to address here are that:

- there have been several attempts to improve the system
- spending has still increased
- criminal defence is still a particular problem.

Important points to include

You should make sure that you are able to include content that deals with each point raised by the quotation:

- Explain the 'several attempts' made to improve the system: remember that there were many Acts of Parliament that took the system from its inception shortly after the Second World War to its current position

- Comment on the first major set of reforms that were introduced by the Access to Justice Act 1999 and the criticisms that were levelled at the system pre-1999 Act: specifically that the costs were increasing rapidly. Increased spending is not a novel problem.

- Discuss the particular reforms that were made by the Access to Justice Act 1999, the CLS and the CDS. Remember that the idea of contracting out to preferred suppliers was designed to keep costs down.

- Consider the operation of the system as it stands – point out that the 1999 reforms excluded certain types of dispute from legal aid, again in a bid to control costs; also mention the role of means testing.

- Look at the role of the CDS and the ways in which the lack of means testing in many situations can result in very large costs to the state; also mention the way in which this was attempted to be managed by the Criminal Defence Service Act 2006.

- Draw reference to the 2010 Green Paper and the changes proposed by the 2011 Bill; consider whether the increased prominence of alternative dispute resolution and the other proposed reforms will finally solve the issues of cost that the earlier programmes of reform seem not to have done.

 Make your answer stand out

Given that this is an area in which there is currently a great deal of change in the pipeline, you should make sure that you are up to date with the current position and current debates. It is always impressive to include something in your answer that shows to your marker that not only do you know the subject well, but that you also are doing something to keep yourself fully informed. If you are revising access to justice, it would be worth checking on the Parliamentary website on the passage of the 2011 Bill and to see if there are any other sources that discuss its ramifications.

READ TO IMPRESS

Bridges, L. *et al.* (2007) *Evaluation of the Public Defender Service in England and Wales,* London: Legal Services.

Lord Carter (2006) *Legal Aid: A Market-based Approach to Reform,* London: HMSO.

Ministry of Justice (2010) *Proposals for the Reform of Legal Aid in England and Wales* (Cm 7967).

www.pearsoned.co.uk/lawexpress

 Go online to access more revision support including quizzes to test your knowledge, sample questions with answer guidelines, podcasts you can download, and more!

And finally, before the exam . . .

By using this revision guide to direct your work, you should now have a good knowledge and understanding of the way in which the various aspects of the English Legal System work in isolation and the many areas in which they overlap or are interrelated. You should also have brushed up the skills and techniques to demonstrate that knowledge and understanding in the examination, regardless of whether the questions are presented to you in essay or problem format.

Test yourself

☐ Look at the **revision checklists** at the start of each chapter. Are you happy that you can now tick them all? If not, go back to the particular chapter and work through the material again. If you are still struggling, seek help from your tutor.

☐ Attempt the **sample questions** in each chapter and check your answers against the guidelines provided.

☐ Go online to **www.pearsoned.co.uk/lawexpress** for more hands-on revision help and try out these resources:

    ☐ Try the **test your knowledge** quizzes and see if you can score full marks for each chapter.

    ☐ Attempt to answer the **sample questions** for each chapter within the time limit and check your answers against the guidelines provided.

    ☐ Listen to the **podcast** and then attempt the question it discusses.

☐ **'You be the marker'** and see if you can spot the strengths and weaknesses of the sample answers.

☐ Use the **flashcards** to test your recall of the legal principles of the key cases and statutes you've revised and the definitions of important terms.

■ Linking it all up

Check where there are overlaps between subject areas. (You may want to review the 'revision note' boxes throughout this book.) Make a careful note of these as knowing how one topic may lead into another can increase your marks significantly. Here are some examples:

✓ Questions on interpretation of statutes or legislation (Chapter 1) can easily link with judicial precedent (Chapter 4) which could then potentially lead further to routes of appeal (Chapters 6 and 7).

✓ The institutions (Chapter 3) are closely related to tribunals and alternative dispute resolution (Chapter 8).

✓ The institutions (Chapter 3) are also very closely linked with the appeals process (Chapters 6 and 7).

■ Knowing your cases

Make sure you know how to use relevant case law in your answers. Use the table below to focus your revision of the key cases in each topic. To review the details of these cases, refer back to the particular chapter.

Key case	How to use	Related topics
Chapter 1 – Legislation and its interpretation		
Sussex	To give a definition of the literal rule	Golden rule, mischief rule
Peerage Case *Grey* v. *Pearson*	To provide a definition of the golden rule	Literal rule, mischief rule

Key case	How to use	Related topics
Pepper v. *Hart*	To show when the courts may refer to *Hansard* as an aid to interpretation	
Chapter 2 – European law		
Van Gend en Loos	To set out the criteria for vertical direct effect of Treaty Articles	
Factortame (No. 2)	To show that there is a presumption that UK statutes are intended to comply with European law	
Chapter 3 – The institutions		
No key cases in this chapter		
Chapter 4 – The doctrine of judicial precedent		
Practice Statement (Judicial Precedent)	To show that the House of Lords (Supreme Court) may depart from its previous decisions 'where it appears right to do so'	
Young v. *Bristol Aeroplane*	Sets out the circumstances in which the Court of Appeal is not bound by its previous decisions	
Chapter 5 – Personnel and the jury system		
No key cases in this chapter		
Chapter 6 – Criminal procedure		
No key cases in this chapter		
Chapter 7 – Civil procedure		
No key cases in this chapter		

▶

Key case	How to use	Related topics
Chapter 8 – Tribunals and alternative dispute resolution		
No key cases in this chapter		
Chapter 9 – Access to justice		
No key cases in this chapter		

■ Sample question

Below is an essay question that incorporates overlapping areas of the law. See if you can answer this question drawing upon your knowledge of the whole subject area. Guidelines on answering this question are included at the end of this section.

ESSAY QUESTION

There is nothing systematic about the English legal system.

Critically analyse this statement.

Answer guidelines

Approaching the question

Before addressing a question such as this, you must be confident that you will be able to demonstrate a range of knowledge and substantiated argument that is both relevant to the statement and sufficiently broad. Remember that the question refers to the English legal system as a whole – which gives you free rein to consider anything you think that is relevant. You will not gain much credit for focusing on one or two areas. Spend some time planning the points that you might want to include. Remember that you are looking for parts of the English legal system that may be 'systematic' (or methodical) and for those parts which may be more unsystematic, unstructured or incoherent.

Important points to include

This question is especially broad and as such it is impossible to give more than an outline indication of some of the points that you might consider in answering it. You would not necessarily be expected to discuss all of the points which follow:

- Discuss what is meant by a legal system.

- Outline the way in which the English legal system operates.

- Compare the operation of the English system with others and note any relevant dif-ferences (European system, US system, cognate Commonwealth jurisdictions).

- Describe the systematic relationship between the institutions of the English legal system. This could include topics such as the hierarchy of the courts, the operation of the doctrine of judicial precedent and the civil and criminal appeals procedure.

- Outline the procedure in civil and criminal cases and discuss how this relates to the system as a whole.

- Evaluate the reform of the tribunals system into something more coherent.

- Consider the common law system and compare and contrast it with the civil law tradition used in other jurisdictions. This could lead on to a further comparison with European law.

- Examine the approaches that are taken towards statutory interpretation by the courts.

 Make your answer stand out

Broad questions such as these are generally marked flexibly and credit is typically given for all and any sensible and reasoned responses. While you would not necessarily be expected to discuss all of the points above, you should certainly explain in relation to each of the points that you do make what it is about that makes it 'systematic' or otherwise. Do not be tempted to describe chunks of the English legal system without some critical analysis of their operation and whether there is scope for deviation from their framework of operation.

A question as wide-ranging as this has no right answer. There is a range of sensible alternative conclusions that could possibly be drawn. You may agree or disagree with the statement in its entirety, or consider that some aspects of the English legal system are systematic and that others are not. You may therefore emphasise those parts of the system that are effective or coherent or those which work less well, or have inconsistencies.

Glossary of terms

The glossary is divided into two parts: key definitions and other useful terms. The key definitions can be found within the chapter in which they occur as well as in the glossary below. These definitions are the essential terms that you must know and understand in order to prepare for an exam. The additional list of terms provides further definitions of useful terms and phrases which will also help you answer examination and coursework questions effectively. These terms are highlighted in the text as they occur but the definition can only be found here.

■ Key definitions

Appeal by way of case stated	A procedure whereby the court against whose decision the appeal is being raised prepares a document for the High Court with a formal request for the opinion of the High Court on whether it was correct in the law and in the application of the law to the facts of that particular case (in other words, the court 'states its case' for consideration by the High Court). The case document will contain the proven facts, the relevant law as understood by the court and the reasons for its decision (in other words, how it applied its understanding of the law to the proven facts in order to reach its conclusion).
Appellant	The party making an appeal.
Burden of proof	The burden of proof lies on the side who has to establish proof.
Case stated	A procedure whereby the court against whose decision the appeal is being raised 'states its case' for consideration by the High Court.

Codifying statute	A statute in which a legal topic, previously contained in the common law, custom and previous statute, is restated (e.g. the Theft Act 1968).
Consolidating statute	A statute in which a legal topic, previously contained in several different statutes, is re-enacted (e.g. the Limitation Act 1980 and the Insolvency Act 1986).
Delegated legislation	Law made by bodies with the authority of Parliament.
Directly applicable	A provision of European law will be directly applicable if it automatically becomes part of the law of a member state without the need for the member state to enact any legislation itself.
Directly effective	A provision of European law will be directly effective if (and only if) it creates rights which individuals may rely upon in their national courts and are enforceable by those courts.
Ejusdem generis	Means 'of the same type'. In other words, if a word with general meaning follows a list of specific words, then the general word applies only to things of the same type as the specific words.
Expressio unius est exclusio alterius	Means that to 'express one thing is to exclude others'; in other words, to list a number of specific things may be interpreted as impliedly excluding others of the same type.
Golden rule	Words must be given their plain, ordinary and literal meaning as far as possible but only to the extent that they do not produce absurdity (narrow approach) or an affront to public policy (wide approach).
Horizontal direct effect	A provision of European law has horizontal direct effect if it can be enforced against another individual.
In camera	Proceedings held in private.
Legislation	A broad term which covers not only statutes (i.e. Acts of Parliament) but other types of legislation such as delegated legislation and European legislation.
Literal rule	Words must be given their plain, ordinary and literal meaning.
Magistrates	The term 'magistrates' encompasses lay magistrates and district judges (magistrates' courts).

Miscarriage of justice	A failure to attain the desired end result of justice.
Mischief rule	The mischief rule involves an examination of the former law in an attempt to deduce Parliament's intention ('mischief' here means 'wrong' or 'harm').
Noscitur a sociis	Means that a word is 'known by the company it keeps'.
Respondent	The party against whom an appeal is being made.
Standard of proof	The required threshold that the proof needs to reach.
Stay	A stay imposes a halt on civil proceedings.
Subordinate legislation	Another term for delegated legislation.
Ultra vires	'Beyond (his) powers'.
Vertical direct effect	A provision of European law has vertical direct effect if it is enforceable against a member state in its own courts. In the United Kingdom this means that vertically directly effective provisions can be enforced against the United Kingdom itself, as well as against local authorities, health authorities and nationalised industries.

■ Other useful terms

Acquittal on indictment	Being found not guilty of an indictable offence.
Appellate	Of or pertaining to appeals.
Article 234 reference	Procedure by which matters of European law requiring a preliminary ruling are brought to the ECJ by member states.
First instance	The first hearing of a case.
Judicial review	Review of the legality of actions of public bodies.
Material facts	Facts which are legally relevant.
Obiter dicta	'Things said in passing'.
Per incuriam	'Through carelessness'.
Preliminary ruling	Clarification provided by the ECJ on interpretation of a particular piece of European legislation.
Puisne judges	High Court judges (*puisne* is pronounced 'puny' and means 'junior').
Questions of law	Questions of law refer to the legal principles of a case, such as the interpretation of a statute.

Questions of fact	Questions of fact relate to the circumstances of the particular case in question.
Ratio decidendi	'The reason for the decision'.
Stare decisis	'Let the decision stand'.

FURTHER READING

If you are in doubt on any legal terminology, you should consult one of the many comprehensive legal dictionaries available. Suitable examples include:

Curzon, L.B. and Richards, P. (2007) *Dictionary of Law*, 7th edn, London: Longman.

Woodley, M. (2009) *Osborn's Concise Law Dictionary* 11th edn, London: Sweet & Maxwell.

Latin phrases and maxims can be found in:

Broom, H. (1939) *A Selection of Legal Maxims: Classified and Illustrated*, 10th edn, London: Sweet & Maxwell (this is also freely available via Google Books).

Judicial definitions can be found in:

Greenberg, D. (2010) *Stroud's Judicial Dictionary of Words and Phrases*, 7th edn, London: Sweet & Maxwell.

Index

INDEX